We Were DECEIVED

DESIREE ALCANTARA

ISBN 978-1-64569-844-9 (paperback)
ISBN 978-1-64569-845-6 (digital)

Christian Faith Publishing, Inc.
832 Park Avenue
Meadville, PA 16335
www.christianfaithpublishing.com

Printed in the United States of America

I want to dedicate this book to my beloved Lord and Savior Jesus Christ/Yeshua Hamashiac. I want to thank Him for saving my soul from the pits of hell and from liberating me from a legion of demons and transforming my life in His light and beauty. I also want to thank my Heavenly Father and the Holy Spirit and to Elohim be all the glory and power. Amen.

I also would like to thank my husband and my son for being there for me and for making my life an amazing journey to enjoy with them. I also want to thank my beautiful niece for all the blessings I received through her life and for the inspiration she gave me. I want to thank my sister, her husband and their beautiful children, who also have blessed my son and me in ways that are beyond wonderful! I would also like to thank my brother and even though we have had rough days and conflicts, I would like to thank him for all the blessings that have come to my life because of him and for all the good memories that we have together. I want to thank all those beautiful people that have touched my life in a special way and changed me for the better and for those who have passed away, I want to honor all of them and hope to see them in heaven someday. Finally, I would like to take this time to thank all those people in my life who tried to oppress me or set me back in life, because it was these people that the Lord used the most to prune my character and to make me more like Him. To Him be all the glory, because everything that happens to those who love the Lord, serves them for good! **Romans 8:28**.

IN A TIME OF UNIVERSAL DECEIT TELLING
THE TRUTH IS A REVOLUTIONARY ACT!
—George Orwell, *1984*

IF LIBERTY MEANS ANYTHING AT ALL,
IT MEANS THE RIGHT TO TELL PEOPLE
WHAT THEY DO NOT WANT TO HEAR.
—George Orwell

THE FURTHER A SOCIETY DRIFTS
FROM TRUTH THE MORE IT WILL
HATE THOSE WHO SPEAK IT.
—George Orwell

WARNING!

You are about to read the truth about our world, and this will become your opportunity to awaken to the truth or if you choose to reject the truth in here, this will become your opportunity to harden your heart drifting further away from the truth. Satan will do everything in his power to try to discredit the truth you will read in this testimony. He will put doubt in your mind, create distractions and interruptions so that you may not finish reading and even discourage you with fear and sadness. We are in a spiritual battle for our souls and eternal lives, and it will be up to you to stand up against the enemy and fight back. It will be your choice to embrace this truth or reject it. Do not take this book lightly, for when everything in this life fades away, all that will remain is the truth. Embrace and accept the truth at all cost, because the truth is what sets you free!

Heavenly Father, I come before Your Presence asking You to please shield and protect the reader of this book and give him or her a clear understanding of all the truth that is in here. I cover them with the blood of the lamb, and I send your angels to protect them from all evil as they venture on reading this material. Please help them to finish reading the whole thing and transform their minds and hearts as they read. This I ask, in the precious name of our Lord Yahushua Hamashiac/Jesus Christ, amen.

For God so loved the world, that He gave His only begotten Son, that whosoever believeth in Him should not perish, but have everlasting life. For God sent not His Son into the world to condemn the world; but that the world through Him might be saved. He that believeth on Him is not condemned: but He that believeth not is condemned already, because he hath not believed in the name of the only begotten Son of God. And this is the condemnation, that light is come into the world, and men loved darkness rather than light, because their deeds were evil. For everyone that doeth evil hateth the light, neither cometh to the light, lest his deeds should be reproved. But he that doeth truth cometh to the light, that his deeds may be made manifest, that they are wrought in God.

—John 3:16–20

AWAKENING

An extravagant night is manifesting a solar-like moon shine, distinguishing from day with the sensual, bright pearl color of night. Along with the silky wind which caresses my skin, between black and white, a blending of my senses promotes me to think. I envisioned the ground to study my shadow inclined, which seems to accompany me even at night. From all directions, thoughts run through my mind, rendering me the sweetest words about life. My house has been blessed as well as the night seems to be, as one enters inside discerning bright colors in peace. Ironically, the full moon's beauty symbolizes the nature of tonight's scenery.

As I claim my senses as evidence to this phenomenon, I feel my spirit arise among momental beats. I'm flowing in flesh as I take this one ride, suddenly "seatbelts" fit comfortably right. Simultaneously, outside my window is an electric connection from relative freedom. Perspectives differ from outside windows, but slowing down only makes me lose rhythm. I cannot stare back for the past is history. Adjacent and heading forward with each flash of glance I absorb, capturing focus believing its mine. Glancing backward sporadically, I emphasize that fuel is adequate, and relative is the inference from the past to the present, enhancing continuum like water in deserts.

Saluting my neighbors meticulously connecting, yet I have to go now my notion motivates me; until the next chance-fate shall bring us together, I will level with you some other time later. So on with my flesh, thoughts and spirit I go; avoiding stagnation to groove with the flow. Wondering thoughts gracefully dance in my head, ending up naked bearing themselves; for they love analyzing from the inside out, rewarding my spirit with stimulating insight. Time out! May I step off the ride unto some concrete please? Conversely, everything seems different now from the outside in. Abstraction embraced me granting me peace, indeed I'm on the ride regardless the location my body may be.

Awareness emphasized my nature of being on an eternal road among soul mates and lessons. Sightings above truth lead a spiritual web and beyond comprehension premium faith says; God has been lovingly guiding my way. Thus, is a long, long ride home my spirit is in, having only death innovating its beats; through the Holy bright light I have been able to see.

Meanwhile, taking down notes with finesse as I cruise all around, concluding my awakening is translating through sound.

Kindred emotions setting me free, allowing my spirit to strengthen my grip. Smoothing adventure thrust into midst and vanity shall not invade my human space for the Lord Jesus Christ protects me from sorrows and pain.

Move over, body! Time to let go the wheel, let the Holy Spirit take over and feel its part heal. Love, wisdom, energy and freedom is the source of my being, adequately keeps me driving in order to be. As my dimension incorporates itself, thrusting eminently, my spirit grows stronger evolving through fate.

INTRODUCTION

"**N**arcissistic Personality Disorder:** A disorder in which a person has an inflated sense of self-importance. The hallmarks of Narcissistic Personality Disorder (NPD) are grandiosity, a lack of empathy for other people, and a need for admiration. People with this condition are frequently described as arrogant, self-centered, manipulative, and demanding." (Article in *Psychology Today*)

CHAPTER 1

THE FEMINIST MOVEMENT

Seems to me that in these modern societies, the majority of people tend to have symptoms of narcissistic personality disorder. I took on the challenge to try to understand the root as to why it is that so many people are suffering with these symptoms; thus, I have done exhaustive research throughout my life to understand the root of what is causing this global epidemic.

According to psychologists, people's personalities are molded throughout their younger years. From the moment a child is born up to the age of seven years old, it is understood by psychologists that a person's personality is majorly developed. Unfortunately, I have come to find that many children across the globe are being raised home alone while parents go out to work.

There is an article in https://www.theguardian.com/world/2016/mar/04/ called "Hidden Crisis of Small Children Left Home Alone While Parents Work." In this article, it states that researchers estimate 35 million children under five years old in the poorest countries are left on their own or with a very young sibling.

By Juliette Jowit, Fri 4 Mar 2016 01.01 EST

Moreover, I have found that it is not only a poor people's problem. It turns out that working, wealthy and middle class, married mothers are also having a very hard time raising their children.

On http://www.dailymail.co.uk/news/article-2678898/ Female-PepsiCo-CEO, there is an article called "Women can't have it all, says Pepsi's mother of-2 boss: Chief says she 'dies with guilt' over compromises she makes to balance career and family life.

Indra Nooyi, 58, made the remarks at this week's Aspen Ideas Festival. She said women 'pretend to have it all' but that it is more an ideal than a reality for most. Nooyi admitted feeling like a bad parent but says she has learned how to feel less guilty. The mother of two was ranked #13 on this year's Forbes list of powerful women."

By Emily Davies Published 00.29 EDT, 3 July 2014.

It is interesting to me to see these articles, since I grew up in a home with both my parents who were married and working. We were a middle-class family. I can remember in my childhood years, that I was left home at a very young age with my siblings who were very young too. Other times we were left with nannies. I remember one of our nanny's was fired because she was caught drugging me with Tylenol so that I can sleep all day while she was with me. I also remember one time where I was alone with some of the kids whom lived near my house. I don't know where any of my parents were or my siblings. I only remember these older kids taking me into a house near mine where another kid who was my same age lived there. They were all older than us. The other kid my age was a boy. We must have been six or seven years old. They told us that they would give us a lot of candy if we took off our clothes and lay on top of each other. We were very young, naïve and totally clueless as to what was happening. I remember we did it. We took off our clothes and I remember the boy and I laid there naked together. There was no intercourse between us, and I don't think I felt I was doing anything wrong up until I noticed that we didn't get any candy, I realized that they had lied to me. I also realized that I felt this great shame and fear that I had never experienced before. They took me home and left. For a long time after that event I was very depressed and felt greatly ashamed. I didn't quite understand what had happened, but I realized that what we did was wrong. No one in my house ever found out about that event.

I am convinced that the event with those kids really molded my character in a major way. I am also sure that the nanny drugging me so that she can relax while taking care of me also molded my character in another major negative way.

Concerning those two articles about a hidden crisis of underage children left home alone while parents work and the article about women not being able to have it all, I not only agree with it one hundred percent, I can relate to them and testify to be true.

My mother was an amazing woman and mother; however, she was by far, way too overloaded with work and responsibilities. There was a time in my life, after I realized all the horrible things that happened to me growing up, that I felt anger toward my mother. I asked myself over and over, why wasn't she there to protect me? Did she not love me? How could she have allowed all these horrible things happen to me? But after becoming a mother myself and understanding the system we are in, I completely understood that it was not her fault. She was set up to fail as a mother and no matter how hard she worked and how many things she did to be a good mother, she was always set up to fail, because the system is rigged and is designed for mothers to fail at raising good children and they are set up to fail to protect them as well.

In wakeupworldnews.com there is an article called "Modern Day Feminism Was Created to Destabilize Society."

It says: "The Feminist movement was devised and conceived by a group of powerful elites decades ago to tear apart the western family values, getting women out working adding half the population to the cash cow for the elites (the tax system) and getting kids into school early to be raised and indoctrinated into the state system, with mum and dad too busy working… This isn't just another conspiracy theory Aaron Russo a highly respected Hollywood director let the cat out of its bag in an interview just before he died."

In https://www.newstatesman.com/politics/feminism/ 2015/10/ there is an article called "Women can't have it all—because the game is rigged."

Work-life balance is a myth. It's time for women to stop blaming themselves and start demanding change. (BY LAURIE PENNY, "FEMINISM," OCTOBER 26, 2015)

Moreover, I see that many people, both women and men, have a real hard time accepting this truth about the feminist movement. To my surprise, Christians also have a very hard time accepting the truth about the feminist movement. I noticed that no matter how much evidence I present to them and how many facts they see, they just simply refuse to accept this as truth. They have been so brainwashed by the indoctrination they received in their schools and in their churches that it seems to me that is almost impossible to prove to them that the feminist movement is evil and that working mothers are being set up to fail.

In http://www.dailymail.co.uk/femail/article-5451309/ is another article called "Psychotherapist warns that working mothers are producing mentally ill children—claims the problem is at an 'epidemic level.'"

Erica Komisar from New York has seen an "epidemic" of mental disorders in clinic. She said young children's stress levels only reduce when their mothers return. She advised working mothers to keep children up late to spend more time together. She said daycare is a stressful environment full of stimulus that's not good for kids.

By SIOFRA BRENNAN FOR MAILONLINE.
PUBLISHED: 04:10 EDT, 2 March 2018

I can vividly remember being a very young child at home and waiting for a very long time for my mother to return from work. I remember I was experiencing a lot of anxiety and fear while waiting for her and when she would come home it would go away.

In https://naturalnews.com/2017-08-27 there is another article called "Over a million children under the age of six are currently on psychiatric drugs in America."

Sunday, August 27, 2017 by: Isabelle Z. Tags: anti-anxiety medication, Antidepressants, antipsychotics, childhood anxiety, childhood depression, psych drugs, psych med alternatives, psychiatric drugs, psychiatric medication, psychiatry. NaturalNews.com.

I have noticed that mental illness in America seems to be a problem that only keeps on growing. Furthermore, the problem is only growing and increasing not because there is no cure, but because we are living in a society that has been artificially engineered to breed mentally ill people. In this book, I intend to prove that there is a conspiracy against humanity and that we have all been deceived! What marvels me the most about this phenomenon is not how cleverly the evil elite have done this, but, how complacent people are and how easily they have allowed themselves to be deceived. It also saddens me deeply to see the level of greed, hardness of hearts and love of money that rules over most of the people; even those whom call themselves followers of Christ.

I need to denote the fact that the church is the one who is responsible that people understand the roles of men and women in society. The church was established by Yeshua Hamashiach /Jesus Christ here on earth to be the place where we learn how to raise our children properly, how to be good husbands and good wives and how to be good, productive citizens of society. But unfortunately, the majority of the church of Jesus Christ is deceived! Christians have allowed many Satanists that were pretending to be Christian ministers to take over roles of leadership in their pulpits and they have twisted the Scriptures and changed the way Christ taught us to function as a society. It is truly disturbing for me to see how many people the enemy has deceived among the body of Christ.

> **"For the time will come when they will not endure sound doctrine; but after their own lusts shall they heap to themselves teachers, having itching ears; And they shall turn away their ears from the truth, and shall be turned unto fables." 2 Timothy 4:3–4**

John Todd was a born-again Christian who exposed a lot of the things the elite were doing. Before he came to the feet of our Lord, he had joined the Illuminati as a young man and served them for many years. He let us know that he personally knew many of the famous Christian preachers of today in America, as Illuminati members. He let us know that he witnessed how they trained these Illuminati servants to become fake Christians and to go into churches and preach a false gospel, they were even working as Christian ministers under the payroll of the Illuminati and many of them are still working for them today disguised as servants of God.

> **Beware of false prophets, which come to you in sheep's clothing, but**

**inwardly they are ravening wolves.
Matthew 7:15**

Once the elite was able to infiltrate the church, they managed to use the church itself to bring about this change upon our society. They managed to twist everything around. What was once a very honorable and respectful role, to be a homemaker…has now changed into being one of the most despicable role a woman in this modern age can have! What was once a very honorable and respectful role, for a husband to be the sole provider and the head of his home, has become an insult and offense to many people of both genders. We have evolved into a society that penalizes masculinity in men and femininity in women. We are so far away from understanding the unique values each gender possess. They managed to strip us from our identities and blind us to the truth about our potentials and beauty of our unique differences. They succeeded in making us believe that we are all created the same and should be doing everything in the same way. Although, we are all equally important and valuable, we are not the same, nor are we supposed to live our lives doing the same things in the same way.

For as the body is one, and hath many members, and all the members of that one body, being many, are one body: so also is Christ. For by one Spirit are we all baptized into one body, whether we be Jews or Gentiles, whether we be bond or free; and have been all made to drink into one Spirit, for the body is

not one member, but many. If the foot shall say, because I am not the hand, I am not of the body; is it therefore not of the body? And if the ear shall say, because I am not the eye, I am not of the body; is it therefore not of the body? If the whole body were an eye, where were the hearing? If the whole were hearing, where were the smelling? But now hath God set the members every one of them in the body, as it hath pleased Him. And if they were all one member, where were the body? But now are they many members, yet but one body. And the eye cannot say unto the hand, I have no need of thee: nor again the head to the feet, I have no need of you. Nay, much more those members of the body, which seem to be more feeble, are necessary: And those members of the body, which we think to be less honourable, upon these we bestow more abundant come- liness. For our comely parts have no need: but God hath tempered the body together, having given more abundant honour to that part which lacked: That there should be no schism in the body; but that the members should have the same care one for another. And whether one member suffer, all the members suffer with it; or one member be hon-

oured, all the members rejoice with it. 1 Corinthians 12:12–26

Men and women were strategically designed and created by God differently so that we balance and edify each other. Just as it is in a team of sports. We were all created to function together as a team. We were never meant to be independent from God or from each other. We all need God and each other and we were created with a limited amount of qualities to specialize in and to use them to serve others, while simultaneously we were meant to receive from others that which they were created with to offer us.

"I am the vine, ye are the branches: He that abideth in Me, and I in him, the same bringeth forth much fruit: for without me ye can do nothing." John 15:5

But the elite who are the ones leading the world, have made us believe that everyone should be working in secular jobs and that it is the "moral way of life," the only way to "serve the family right," and that is the "ethical thing to do." They have made us believe that everyone paying taxes is the only way society can flourish and prosper. They have brainwashed the masses about this, and the people have completely forgotten that once upon a time, women stayed home and homeschooled their children and the men were the sole providers and it actually worked well for them.

"The aged women likewise, that they be in behavior as becometh holiness, not false accusers, not given to much wine, teachers of good things; that they may teach the young women to be sober, to love their husbands, to love their children, to be discreet, chaste, keepers at home (homemakers) good, obedient to their own husbands, that the word of God be not blasphemed."
Titus 2:3–5

The deception has been so massive that we now live in a society that condemns homemakers as people who are lazy, incompetent, unintelligent, irresponsible, leaches and they even go as far as to accuse them of stealing from the government because of not paying taxes. We live in a society that preaches this message to the masses from their church pulpits and feel absolutely no remorse about it because they genuinely believe that they are right. They have no concerns about what is going on with that child that is being left home alone under the age of five, being exposed to all kinds of dangers or that teenager who is not being supervised and exposed to all sorts of temptations. They have no concern that children are spending hours and hours behind a screen getting fed pure garbage that is murdering their spirit. They don't consider that all that time that the child is alone, he is unprotected, left to predators to do to them whatever evil they desire, they don't consider that they are afraid, with no guidance, no love or affection, no one there to serve them food and keep them warm and peaceful.

They only think and talk about the part that the mother needs to go out and work and pay taxes so that she can be "productive" and "holy."

That is as silly and foolish as a soccer team playing a game where the goal keeper is peer pressured into going to the front lines and play next to the striker, because back in the goal post, the goal keeper "seems" to be doing nothing productive most of the time.

This is how silly and foolish these nations that have bought this feminist movement ideology are! They have fallen for the trap to abandon their children, so that the elite can devour them and train them to become the way they want them to be. Is a brilliant plan I must say! If I was the devil and I wanted to destabilize society and the family structure, the first thing I would do, would be to take the mother away from the children as long and as far as possible. This way, the children are as most vulnerable and ignorant as they can be. The rest is a piece of cake!

In http://www.healthy-holistic-living.com/family-life-stress.html there is an article that states, "Studies Show That Husbands Stress Women Twice As Much As Children." This is what would happen to a goal keeper that is sent to the front lines to play as a striker, but is also expected to never allow the other team score a goal against them back in the goal post.

In general, women are being exploited and overloaded with work and responsibilities and don't have the help they need to accomplish getting everything done right. Men were designed by God to be protectors and providers. They were designed by God to go out and work. They were not designed by God to focus most of their attention and energy in educating and counseling their children or cooking meals for the kids at the home and cleaning up after them. Even though some men do this full time, in general most men do not do this type of things nor do they enjoy doing them; or have the patience to do them. But most women have more grace than men to do those types of things, because they are designed by God to do this type of things.

Unto the woman He said, I will greatly multiply thy sorrow and thy conception; in sorrow thou shalt bring forth children; and thy desire shall be to thy husband, and he shall rule over thee. Genesis 3:16

And unto Adam He said, because thou hast hearkened unto the voice of thy wife, and hast eaten of the tree, of which I commanded thee, saying, Thou shalt not eat of it: cursed is the ground for thy sake; in sorrow shalt thou eat of it all the days of thy life; Thorns also and thistles shall it bring forth to thee; and thou shalt eat the herb of the field; in the sweat of thy face shalt thou eat bread, till thou return unto the ground; for out of it wast thou taken: for dust thou art, and unto dust shalt thou return. And Adam called his wife's name Eve; because she was the mother of all living. Genesis 3:17–20

To Adam He said to go out to work and to Eve He said: "Be a mother…"

People need to understand that staying at home is a full-time job. Raising children and caring for the husband is a full-time job. But this society believes that is not important to invest time with the children and that marriages can work even though both partners are too busy working to spend much quality time together. It amazes me to see how so many intelligent and educated people out there don't see how silly it is to think that we can raise healthy, sound minded and emotionally intelligent children without giving them the proper amount of affection, attention and love that they need. It amazes me how people believe that we can have strong marriages without investing a lot of time together, cultivating that love. We live in an era where people have become utterly delusional.

Technology has replaced human interaction with each other. Since the moment children come into the world, they have IPads and laptops on their hands. There is an article in https://nypost.com/2016/08/27 titled: "It's a digital heroin': How screens turn kids into psychotic junkies. By Dr. Nicholas Kardaras August 27, 2016. In this article it speaks about all the harmful effects all these technologies have on children. It truly is mind boggling how harmful these things are for them. Yet here we are… Living in a world, where most parents, male and females work forty to sixty hours per week and are too tired from work when they are home to emotionally engage well with their young children; thus they substitute the attention and service to their kids with technology and the media who is also full of violence and sexual perversion. Furthermore, there is an article in www.independent.co.uk/science titled: "Study finds that violent video games may be linked to aggressive behavior." It goes on to say that "Violent video games are a 'risk factor' for increased aggression. Written by: John von Radowitz, Press Association/ Monday 17 August 2015 08.59 BST.

In addition, in https://www.telegraph.co.uk/news/science/11087683/ there is an article called "Watching violent films does make people more aggressive, study shows." In the first study of its kind, researchers found that each person's reaction depended on how aggressive they were to begin with. Violence on screen can translate into real life, according to a new study Photo: Alamy. By: Keith Perry, and agency 6:00 p.m. BST 10 Sep 2014.

It really disturbs me to see so many smart people wonder; "Why is our world so messed up?" How can it not be messed up, when we have removed homemakers out of the home and replaced them with artificial intelligence, technology that is just like drugs and media that is sending out messages of pure filth, violence, sexual perversion and all kinds of abominations? How can anyone think that this way of life will turn out right for us as a whole?

"The light of the body is the eye: If therefore thine eye be single, thy whole body shall be full of light. But if thine eye be evil, thy whole body shall be full darkness. If therefore the light that is in thee be darkness, how great is that darkness!" Matthew 6:22–23

When I was a teenager, I watched a lot of violence and sexual perversion in the TV and heard music that was aggressive and sexually explicit as well. My parents were Catholics and even though we were raised in the Catholic Church, it was quite normal to indulge ourselves in entertainment that was extremely unholy. Moreover, I remember all my teenage friends also indulging in the same way as I did with these types of entertainment. I never met anyone during my teenage years that was a true Christian and that was living a holy life style. Thus, I thought it was perfectly normal to sit down and watch sexually explicit films or music videos or horror and violent films, no one ever told me it was bad for me. I thought it was normal to dress provocative and dance sensually to music that was sexually explicit. And most of my friends, (which were many of them), were just like me in that aspect.

Growing up, I was a pretty wild child to say the least. I enjoyed playing sports and hanging out with lots of friends. I started drinking beers at thirteen years old. I hung out with lots of kids who got drunk since they were ten, eleven, and twelve years old. I started going into eighteen years old and older type of clubs in Miami Beach, FL, when I was only fourteen years old. I was always so hungry for adventure and I chased adrenalin highs like a drug. My friends began smoking pot since we were teenagers, but for some strange reason, I made the decision to not smoke any marijuana, no matter how much peer pressure I received by friends to do so. I said no to pot, hundreds of times, again and again, for years…leaving my friends in a state of wonder as to why I didn't want to smoke. I don't really know if part of it had to do, that I saw how much they desired that

I try it, and the more they would try to convince me into doing it, the rebellion within me compelled me to say no!

My friends were pretty wild kids! Some of them were too wild, but even though I did not do the crimes they would do, I still would hang out with them. I had a friend in the seventh grade who was in gangs. He got into a dispute with his ex-girlfriend one day and shot her to death and turned the shot gun unto himself and killed himself. I will never forget that event or his funeral. It marked me for life! I had friends that would break into houses and steal people's belongings and they would steal cars and just take them out for "joy rides" and then throw them in lakes to hide the evidence. I had friends that were tripping on LSD and trying all kinds of drugs. However, when hanging out with them, I would just stick with drinking lots of beers. I had a sense of respect concerning using drugs. I felt it was not wise. Thus, throughout middle school and high school, miraculously, I never smoked pot or touched any drugs, even though everyone in my circle of friends were using drugs. However, I think I compensated my not getting high on drugs with drinking lots of beers and alcohol. I used to even out drink some of the toughest male drinkers within my crowd sometimes. I also smoked cigarettes as a social smoker, from time to time. The one thing all of my friends and I had most in common was this one thing: "Most of all of us had no adults in our homes to supervise what we were doing." Most of us had our parents at work while we were doing all these crazy things during the weekdays after school.

We were not raised by our parents. We were being indoctrinated by our school educational system which is totally sold out to the agenda that the Elite have for a One World Order, and their agenda includes dumbing down the children and converting them into obedient slaves to the bank system. There is a leaked video on YouTube called "Illuminati Training Video Leaked" where they show you all the things they have worked on to destroy us and one of them was how they took over the educational system.

Hence, the indoctrination with my friends and I would continue when we would come out of school and enter a demonic trance listening to music that had been anointed by Satan to mind control us. John Todd also speaks about how Satanists do rituals before recording music and send demons to the records, so that when we are listening to this music those demons take a hold of our minds and souls. He exposes the truth about how these musicians sold their souls to Satan for fame and money and how they are being used to mind control the masses.

Then we were being indoctrinated much more the moment we would turn on our TVs. There's a documentary in YouTube called *Hollywood Actors Exposed, full documentary* by a Christian man named Dr. Jason Kovar, a man who was aspiring to become an actor, but instead God pulled him out of Hollywood and is now using him to expose the truth about Hollywood. In this documentary, he exposes the truth about how most of these actors are serving Satan. They channel and invoke demons before doing their films and he clearly shows that truly demons are using Hollywood to infiltrate the homes of Christians and take possession of their souls.

When I come across women who are mothers and have jobs outside their homes for forty to sixty hours per week and they tell me how they believe they are the ones raising their children and "doing it all" I can't help but wonder if they are delusional or self-deceived? I am sorry to say, but no, full-time working mothers are not raising their children when they are being sent to be indoctrinated in schools for forty to sixty hours per week and then they are being indoctrinated by their technology and media the rest of their time. In my personal experience growing up and after all the research I have done, I have to say that most parents are not raising their children at all. They may be financially providing for them all their basic needs and some, but concerning their spiritual lives, emotional and mental health, those important areas are being majorly neglected by most parents.

God led me to see an interview with a serial killer named Ted Bundy. In his last interview, right before he was executed, he confessed that he grew up in a very loving Christian home. He was loved by his parents and four siblings. He had a nice home and they were a typical American Christian family. He went to church every Sunday, was sent to the best schools where he earned good grades and a lawyer's degree. He was liked by everyone in his life. But he had a serious problem. At the age of twelve years old, he was "left home alone" a lot. He would watch pornography during his time at home when no one was watching him. He also watched very violent movies and he got addicted to it. Unfortunately, he became a serial rapist and a murderer and a monster as a result of it. He talked about how people were criticizing his parents, but he said, he didn't understand why they would criticize his parents, when now a days, most parents leave their underage children home alone to go to work all the time. He said the same way he was raised it's how most children in America are being raised. Most of these kids are spending their time the same way Ted Bundy was. Perhaps, some of them may never become killers, but nevertheless, this is no way to raise children people, we must wake up!

CHAPTER 2

MY TESTIMONY

High school for me was a pretty wild ride! I partied so hard throughout my high school years. I loved dancing and playing soccer, volleyball and basketball. I met lots of people and loved to hang out with all kinds of kids. I went to the beach religiously, during the day time I was in the ocean and during the night time I was in the clubs almost every weekend. I even worked promoting different parties at clubs and hosting the parties in the club. I did some modeling on the side and loved to work out in the gym. I had made so many friends and I truly felt as if I was on top of the world. I was very outgoing and super happy and sociable most of the time. I had a few boyfriends, but none of them lasted for too long because even though I was pretty wild, I was actually saving myself for the right guy. Even though I flirted a lot with guys and dressed provocatively, I did not sleep around with men. Thus, once my boyfriends would see that I did not wish to go "all the way with them" they would not want to continue dating me.

Thus, I was single most of my time during my high school years.

I had lots of hobbies, but the most peculiar hobby I had was writing in my journals. I began writing when I was fourteen years old. I wrote about everything! I wrote daily about my daily activities. But I also loved to analyze life, people and my own self in my writings. I was so curious about why we were here on earth, about what is our purpose in life and what happens after we die. I was so curious to discover the meaning of it all! I thought that if I searched within my soul and mind through the pen and paper, somehow I would figure it all out! I spent hours and hours writing in my journals. I sort of became obsessed with writing. I would lose track of time and write so much that my hand would get tired to the point of feeling injured. I used to have to put ice on my right hand, because of how much it hurt and then I would go back to my journal.

Even though I was having a lot of fun throughout my teenage years, I was also experiencing pretty dark circumstances. The death of my seventh-grade friend really impacted my life. Shortly before his death, my uncle had also died, and his funeral also marked my life. I would wonder where they were. I could not help but think that they were still somewhere and not completely cut off from existence. I sometimes thought that their spirits were actually roaming around me. I would write about it in my journals.

I would also write about my heartache from losing my boyfriends. Whether I broke up with them or they broke up with me, it was always devastating for me. I guess I was vulnerable and fragile in my emotions, but I didn't know why? Now I do. But back then, I didn't. I would go into deep depressions and found my escape in my journals.

The more I wrote, the hungrier for knowledge I would get. I began reading books of all kinds. Books about reincarnation, about hypnotism, etc… I read so many different types of books except the Bible. For some strange reason, I just could not read the Bible. It bored me to death and I also could not really understand it. I was raised Catholic and my Catholic Elementary School instilled in me the habit to pray to God every day. I also learned some things from the Bible through them, but not a lot. Thus, I was searching for the truth in all the wrong places. I went to psychics to tell me my future and tarot card readers, I went to witches and I would sit down with religious people from all kinds of religions to hear what they had to say. But I was not satisfied, I wanted to learn the truth and I wanted to fill my void inside my heart, and so far, nothing that I had been doing was ever enough. On the contrary, the more I read and wrote, the further from the truth I was getting and deeper into darkness. Just as how we get drifted away in the ocean by the subtle current, I was drifting away from God and His truth more and more each day without knowing it.

I began to believe all sorts of lies. Philosophies and demonic doctrines were the ones dominating my mind. I began to fall in love with the supernatural, but it was a dark spiritual realm that I was entering into without knowing it.

Beware lest any man spoil you through philosophy and vain deceit, after the tradition of men, after the

rudiments of the world, and not after Christic. Colossians 2:8

In my junior year of high school, my beloved mother was diagnosed with breast cancer. She was given six months to live. I was devastated by this! Everyone in my family was too. My older sister, my younger brother and my father were all devastated by this news. My mom tried to get into a holistic type of treatment to try to defeat the cancer, but even though she began eating different, she still went ahead and did the chemotherapies that they said she had to do. I was the one who would drive her most of the time to the hospital to do those chemotherapy sessions. It was extremely painful for me. Every time she would go, she would come back feeling horrible. She would throw up black vomit all over the carpet and I would clean it up. She would get really cold and the next moment she was really hot. She would be in pain and agony. I used to have to give her full body massages so that she may feel a little bit better, because her bones would hurt greatly. She would complain and say that she felt as if she was on fire inside. She became so disabled, that I had to bathe her and take her to the bathroom all the time. She became like a child and I became her mother.

I literally became her full-time nurse. Even though they had given her six months to live; she actually lived three years more. But oh boy, did she suffer through those years. I saw her transition from this absolutely gorgeous and healthy looking woman, into a very ill and old looking woman. Her eyebrows and hair fell off, one of her breasts was amputated, she began to lose weight and get dry and wrinkled skin and she even shrunk a little bit from her height. I began taking care of her in my junior year in high school and by my senior year, her illness began taking a huge toll on my emotional and mental health.

I graduated in 1994 and in February 9, 1995 a friend of mine was killed in a car accident. I was deeply wounded by this event. I don't know if it was that I was already extremely emotionally vulnerable because of my mother's illness, or if it was that my boyfriend of seven months had recently broken up with me, or if it was all the other bad things that had been happening to me. But by the end of my high school years, I was convinced that I was cursed. Even though I would party a lot and have lots of fun, a lot of bad things were always happening to me at the same time. I broke three ligaments on my right foot while working out in the gym and I had to be on a cast for seven months and I had been experiencing a lot of supernatural scary events which were making me believe that I was being haunted by ghosts and that someone did witchcraft on me. So when I heard the news about my friend dying in a car accident, and how a drunk driver hit him as he was trying to fix his girlfriend's car in the expressway, I was plunged into a full-blown depression!

Writing about it all was my portal into a different reality which brought me some sort of comfort from all the pain. I would dive into my own mind and come out of it, hours and hours later. What felt to me as a couple of hours of sitting down writing had actually transitioned into more than seven or eight hours of nonstop writing. It was like if I would go into a trance. I would feel like if I would get high from writing. I began experimenting writing with trance like music in the background and that surely did take me into a much higher level. The more I would write about all the supernatural spooky experiences that were happening to me and around me, the more intense those experiences would get. I didn't know if my writing about those things were causing more of those types of things to occur, but I felt it did have something to do with it. I began to sort of go on a ghost hunting type of journey through my writings, but just as Alice in Wonderland, I feel I was too consumed by chasing this rabbit down the hole and definitely, I followed him way down there and just as it happened to her, I also got lost. Extremely lost!

I experienced the same type of phenomenon that the movie called "Fallen" with actor Denzel Washington from 1998, is all about.

In 1996, my beautiful niece was born in September, my grandmother died in October 30, my mother died in December, Friday the thirteenth and I was institutionalized in the Miami Jackson Mental Health Hospital with a diagnosis of psychoaffective chronic schizophrenia. 1996 was an unforgettable year for me. This year was the end of my world! But it also was the year I was born again in Christ.

I went through pure hell on earth and it forever changed the course of my life!

Be not deceived; God is not mocked: for whatsoever a man soweth, that shall he also reap. Galatians 6:7

Behold, I set before you this day a blessing and a curse; A blessing, if ye

obey the commandments of the Lord your God, which I command you this day: And a curse, if ye will not obey the commandments of the Lord your God, but turn aside out of the way which I command you this day, to go after other gods, which ye have not known. Deuteronomy 11:26–28

When thou art come into the land which the Lord thy God giveth thee, thou shalt not learn to do after the abominations of those nations. There shall not be found among you any one that maketh his son or his daughter to pass through the fire, or that useth divination, or an observer of times, or an enchanter, or a witch, or a charmer, or a consulter with familiar spirits, or a wizard, or a necromancer. For all that do these things are an abomination unto the Lord: and because of these abominations the Lord thy God doth drive them out from before thee. Thou shalt be perfect with the Lord thy God. Deuteronomy 18:9–13

But it shall come to pass, if thou wilt not hearken unto the voice of the Lord thy God, to observe to do all His commandments and His statutes which

I command thee this day; that all these curses shall come upon thee, and overtake thee:

So that thou shalt be mad for the sight of thine eyes which thou shalt see. Deuteronomy 28:15, 34

In 1996, the verdict against me from heaven was out! At nineteen years old I found myself reaping all the iniquity I had sown throughout my entire life. I found myself guilty on front of a Holy God. Judgment day had arrived at my door and swept me off my feet brutally! It seemed as if all the curses from the Bible were being launched against me one after another without giving me time to recuperate from the previous one. I did not know I was doing so much evil! I thought I was a good person. I thought that God was proud of me and that I was doing my best. But I was proven wrong by an Almighty God, Who's wrath was poured out upon me like a tsunami from the ocean.

There is a way which seemeth right unto a man, but the end thereof are ways of death. Proverbs 14:12

For the wages of sin is death, but the gift of God is eternal life through Jesus Christ our Lord. Romans 6:23

This I say then, walk in the Spirit, and ye shall not fulfill the lust of the flesh. For the flesh lusteth against the

Spirit, and the Spirit against the flesh: and these are contrary the one to the other: so that ye cannot do the things that ye would. But if ye be led of the Spirit, ye are not under the law. Now the works of the flesh are manifest, which are these; Adultery, fornication, uncleanness, lasciviousness, idolatry, witchcraft, hatred, variance, emulations, wrath, strife, seditions, heresies, envyings, murders, drunkenness, revellings, and such like: of the which I tell you before, as I have told you in time past, that they which do such things shall not inherit the kingdom of God. Galatians 5:16–21

Thus, even though I was thinking to myself I was "righteous," because I was nice to my friends and family and because I was caring and helping people from time to time with their problems. I was unaware that I was committing all those sins mentioned here in the Bible, again and again, day by day. I was utterly blinded to the fact that I was constantly crucifying Jesus Christ in my life without knowing how much I was hurting my Savior whom died for me. I was guilty of it all and the conviction about it came upon my heart like thunder and lightning in 1996.

In 1996, I believe I had a taste of hell and I also believe that in this year I met Satan face to face. Satan revealed himself to me greatly during this time and I got a front row seat to observe his evil and slick tactics against humanity. He is a master deceiver indeed and a charismatic con artist.

Be sober, be vigilant; because your adversary the devil, as a roaring lion, walketh about, seeking whom he may devour! 1 Peter 5:8

Lest Satan should get an advantage of us: for we are not ignorant of his devices. 2 Corinthians 2:11

Finally, my brethren, be strong in the Lord, and in the power of His might. Put on the whole armor of God, that ye may be able to stand against the wiles of the devil. For we wrestle not against flesh and blood, but against principalities, against powers, against the rulers of the darkness of this world, against spiritual wickedness in high places. Ephesians 6:10–12

A Covenant of Love

Elohim: Supreme power, sovereignty and glory. Nothing is impossible for Elohim. It means I am the true God. Sometimes it is plural, as "In the beginning God…" (Genesis 1:1) Elohim means I am the God of trinity-God the Father, God the Son, and God the Holy Spirit. The word also implies that I am God of several powers, many resources, many majesties, much glory, and absolute authority. By the power of My word I formed the worlds. I brought order out of chaos. I still do. I am Omnipotent, the God of power. Because of My great love, I use My power on behalf of My children. Elohim-Hebrew word. I am your God Almighty. Another Hebrew word is El-Shaddai. The word means the ever-existent One, the Eternal, the One continually revealing Himself, His ways, His purposes. Nothing is impossible with El-Shaddai. Nothing is too hard for Me. When you need Me, I am present to help you, to sustain you, to nourish you. The Psalmist knew Me as his El-Shaddai. He said: "It is God who arms me with strength and makes my way perfect" (Psalm 18:32). What I did for the psalmist I am able to do for you. I am the all-sufficient God, the all bountiful God. I abundantly bless My children. My resources are inexhaustible. My child: You are not your own. You have been bought with a price, the blood of Jesus Himself. Honor Him in all your decisions and you will be blessed!

(Passage was from the book: "God Can Heal Your Heart" by Marie Shropshire)

Jesus, will You marry me? My precious King; You have taught me the value of my life in many mysterious ways. I would like to take this time to thank You for all my happiness. I walked the darkest valleys any human being can possibly imagine. I now can clearly see how not for one split second, You never, ever stopped loving me. As I felt lost in despair, frustration and confusion, I literally drowned in an ocean of fear. Hopeless and restless, I roamed without solution. Seconds feeling like an eternity, were eating me up inside. Slowly disintegrating, my soul was feeling trapped. Captured by the devil's tricks, I panicked with nowhere to hide. Secluded from this planet, was what made me realize, that without Your Holy Spirit, there is absolutely no point or meaning to life.

As demons walked me through the halls of hell, I faced the enemy face to face. I learned just how real the devil is and I do thank You Lord for allowing this experience to happen to me. For I believe in You with such great faith and soon this world's nightmare will fade away. I know the fairytale the future holds for me and it's not a dream, it's my reality. I feel so blessed that You chose me to live this bizarre life You granted me. I assure You Lord that my love for You will only grow stronger beat by beat. I feel as a soldier fighting a battle of negative vibes, only succeeding with You by my side. Falling in love with Your Holiness, my spirit hungers to kill my flesh. Aparting sins from my life is what I long and desire; help me Jesus Christ to keep myself sanctified. I would love to take You as my Spiritual Husband, for I feel as we're soulmates as soon as I accepted You in my heart. Thank You my love for all that You have done for me. Bless the planet earth and set all of us free. Send Your battle of angels from heaven above to guide us down here so deep. Deep in darkness is where most people live, please dear Lord help every single soul that is lost find the light. In the name of Jesus I pray and give You thanks. Amen!

(Written by Desiree Carrasquillo in 1998)

CHAPTER 3

THE MENTAL INSTITUTION

It was a calm evening at my home. Both my parents were there, and I had been out of the house all day. When I got home that evening, I entered my home and saw my father, but I was not well. I was hallucinating. My father's face looked like the last boyfriend that had recently broken up with me. Then I saw my mother and she also did not really look like her. She looked like the girl that dated my ex-boyfriend right before I was in his life. I became infuriated! I thought it was no longer my parents, but my ex-boyfriend with his ex-girlfriend. I completely lost sense of reality! I began to scream at them in pure rage and they just watched me in pure horror! I was so upset, I began to pace back and forth in my living room like a mad woman. I went to the stereo and put my Nine Inch Nails CD that I used to have. I put the volume all the way up and I began to sing out loud the lyrics of the song as if I was possessed! From the top of my lungs, I began to sing: "Don't take it away from me, I need someone to hold on to… Don't take it away from me, I need someone to hold on to" "Terrible

Lies," and on and on I kept on singing to the lyrics to this satanic band that I used to love…and every single word in those songs seem to relate to my feelings and emotions so deeply, it was comforting to me.

Thus, as I was getting lost in my singing and releasing all my stress at the expense of my poor parents; suddenly, two very tall men in uniform came into my home and interrupted my performance. I noticed that my mom was in her bed crying and one of the police men was there talking to her. I snapped out of my delusion and realized my mom was there and that she was crying. Then I decided to go in her room to check up on her and the police man stops me on my tracks. Thus, I took all my rage out on him and tackled him down unto the floor just like a football player does to his opponent on a field. These men were both above six feet tall and it seemed to matter nothing to me. I was fearless and reckless and full of rage! I suddenly found myself sitting down in the back of the police car with hand cuffs on and on my way to somewhere. I began to sing again, the song from the movie *Natural Born Killers*: "I guess I was boooornn, naturally booornn, born BAD! Born BAD is such a SIN! I guess I was boooorn, naturally born, born baaaaddd!" As my house faded away from my sight, I can hear the police men laughing while I sang.

As I entered the mental institution, all I can remember is that I had like five men trying to calm me down and could not hold me still. I was fighting them all. Until after a pretty long struggle with them, they injected something into me and strapped me down. I was placed in an isolated room far away from all the other rooms and there was only a very small window on my door. I was strapped unto the bed of this horrible place all night long. I remember feeling as if I had been buried alive. I cried all night long and begged for someone to help me out of there. I urinated on myself and believe it or not, I thought about Jesus Christ that moment. I thought about Him being crucified unto the cross and having to endure staying that way for a long time without being able to move any part of his body. I was strapped with my arms spread apart from each other and I was in an extremely uncomfortable position. That was by far the worse night of my life. I felt that room was my coffin and that I would be there forever. It was pure torture!

They diagnosed me with chronic schizophrenia. They told my parents I was never going to be healed or normal again and that I would have to live for the rest of my life under psychiatric meds and they told my father that I should be in the institution all of my life because I was a threat to society and to myself. I was only nineteen years old, but I was placed in the section were the adults over forty years old were, because of how bad I was.

Thankfully for me, my father chose to take me out of there without obeying their advice. He signed an affidavit making himself responsible for my life and whatever I would do. He took me out of there and took care of me like if I was a baby. I was invited to a church where they practiced liberation of demons and sure enough, I had demons. A legion of them and they were cast out by the leaders of this very small church where I was taken into.

I will never forget that night. I entered this very small church in the middle of a shopping center. They were starting their service with worship and praise music playing from the altar. I felt the hairs of my body rise everywhere. I did not comprehend what it was that I was experiencing. I felt this incredible power coming upon me. It was making me extremely uncomfortable. I began to think to myself that I needed to get out of that place. I visualized myself running out of there and never coming back. But to my own surprise, I ran unto the altar instead and threw myself on the floor on my knees. I could not believe I was hearing myself begging God to rescue me. I said: "God please, liberate me from this torment, I cannot bear it any longer!" Then I heard a very deep sound coming out my mouth. It was a very creepy and scary sound. It was a demon. A couple of them started to scream out from my body. I could no longer find my voice. All I was hearing was strange voices and screams coming out of me. Moreover, the leaders decided to cancel the church service, and everyone left the church that night, except the leaders, the people who brought me there and someone else who thought he should stay.

> **Behold, I give unto you power to tread on serpents and scorpions, and over all the power of the enemy and nothing shall by any means hurt you. Luke 10:19**

They sat me down in a chair and surrounded me, they were praying and anointing me with oil. I was out of control. I wanted to punch them all. I felt so much hate toward them. I can still remember those feelings. But as I was closing my fists to try to punch them, they began to ordain me in the name of Jesus Christ to keep my hands down and to not touch anyone or harm my own self. I then felt as if an angel grabbed my arms and held them down to the chair. Even though I was trying my hardest to raise my arms and even though no one was grabbing me any longer, I could not move any part of my body. I was binded to that chair just as they commanded in the name of Jesus and I could not understand how.

> **And these signs shall follow them that believe; In My name shall they cast out devils; they shall speak with new tongues; they shall take up serpents and if they drink any deadly thing, it shall not hurt them; they shall lay hands on the sick, and they shall recover. Mark 16:17–18**

They started to name demon after demon, and the demons started to manifest and come out. When each demon would be mentioned, I would experience their emotion and then I would feel them leave my body. I remember feeling inside of my womb as if they were ripping me apart. Because they were. They were holding onto my womb trying to stay inside me. I felt pain inside of my womb for many months after my liberation that day. I had arrived at that place at 8:00 p.m. that night and that was when I went to the altar, it was 4:00 a.m. when it all ended. We were all exhausted and completely shocked and amazed at what just happened. That night I was never the same again. I feel I birthed my own self. I saw the power of God and the power of Satan at its best. God is more powerful by far!

I remember that whenever they put oil on my skin, I felt as if I was getting burned. This whole experience was too real for me. No one can ever convince me that there is no God or no devil. I became determined to know the Lord and to repent and to bring as many souls to God as possible. I also knew that the Bible warns you that if you have demons cast out of your life and if you continue to practice sin, they will come back with seven stronger ones for each one that left. Thus, I was not going to take any chances on that ever happening to me. I was going to make sure those evil creatures never, ever come back in me and that I would always overcome them in the name of Jesus Christ/ Yeshua Hamashiach.

I studied the Scriptures day and night. Thankfully, my pastors were very dedicated to me and helped me a lot. They had much to do with my healing, because they invested hours and hours in teaching me the Word of God and fasting and praying for me. They taught me everything there is to know about spiritual warfare. I learned to fast and do spiritual intercession. I went to their services which were every day, since 8:00 p.m. to 10:30 p.m. and sometimes we would come out much later. My pastor was a walking Bible. He knew the Scriptures by heart, and he would recite them repeatedly. His sermons were not like most sermons which you hear a couple of verses and a bunch of words from men. NO, he was the opposite. His sermons were a bunch of verses and very few of his own words. I think I have never met a preacher as anointed as this man was and as gifted in the teaching of the word of God as he was. I was truly very blessed to have landed in that church. He and his wife both had been into witchcraft before coming to the feet of our Lord and they were trained by God in liberating people who were in the occult as they were. They both took me into their life almost as their daughter.

> And when he was come to the other side into the country of the Gergesens, there met him two possessed with devils, coming out of the tombs, exceeding fierce, so that no man might pass by that way. And, behold, they cried out, saying: "What have we to do with thee, Jesus, thou Son of God?" Art thou come hither to torment us before the time? And there was a good way off from them an herd of many swine feeding. So the devils besought him, saying, if thou cast us out, suffer us to go away into the herd of swine. And He said unto them, Go. And when they were come out, they went into the herd of swine: and behold, the whole herd of swine ran violently down a steep place into the sea, and perished in the waters. And they that kept them fled, and went their ways into the city, and told everything and what was befallen to the possessed of the devils. And behold, the whole city came out to meet Jesus and when they saw Him, they besought him that he would depart out of their coasts. Matthew 8:28–34

CHAPTER 4

My Niece

In 1996, my mother and grandmother passed away and my niece was born. Aside from the unconditional love my Heavenly and earthly father gave me, the love and support from certain family members and friends and aside of the prayers and support the church gave me, my niece was a great part of my liberation and healing process. I thank my Lord Yeshua Hamashiach for having blessed me with such a precious little princess in the darkest hour of my life. I truly don't know what would have happened to me, had it not been for Hailie (Not her real name).

She was born a few months prior to my mother's death. I was utterly depressed, and I had absolutely no desire to live anymore. I did not have the motivation to do anything. I was so physically still for so long that my left leg literally began to fail me. My sister had to help me learn to walk all over again and I remember dragging my left leg as I was starting to get out of the house and walk again. I had been paralyzed by fear and sadness. Literally paralyzed! To the point that I remember I spent most of my time in my mother's bed, rocking back and forth in a fetus position, in absolute fear, panic and sadness. My father used to ask me to hold the baby in my arms as she slept so that I can experience the joy that it feels to do that. But I would always tell him no. But he always insisted that I carry her, and he would force me to hold her. He would sit me down in his rocking chair and place her in my arms and once that sweet baby was there, I could not resist! I would feel my heart just melting away and all that anger and hardness was slowly fading away, by the warmth of her love and innocence...

Suddenly, it became our new routine in 1996–1998. I would sit down, and he would hand her over to me and she would sleep on my chest while my heart just melted by watching her sleep. The love that she imparted upon me as she slept on my arms was indescribable! In the middle of all my inner torment and chaos, here came this angel and brightened up my life in a way I never imagined was possible. My younger brother is her father and he and his girlfriend whom also lived with us had her when they were teenagers. After Hailie was eight months old, her mother moved back to Georgia where she was from, but Hailie stayed with us. I became her full-time mother. My brother and father worked and paid the bills and I stayed home and took care of her. At first, two of my best friends and one of my cousin's, were always taking care of her too. Also, my father hired a nanny from Costa Rica and had her move in with us to care for Hailie. But she wasn't there long because our house was way too chaotic for anyone to handle it. Thus, during 1996 to 1998, there were many hands taking care of Hailie. But it eventually evolved into me being the main person that would take care of her.

It turned out that even though I never really signed up to become a real mother at the age of nineteen and twenty, I had no saying in the matter. There was no one there but me and Hailie most of the time. It just turned out to be a great blessing for me. The more time I spent with her, the better I was feeling. She gave me a new sense of hope and life. A new desire and motivation to live. I wanted to have the house clean for her. I wanted to give her a good time just because seen her smile became my reward. Her being there just gave me the determination I needed to fix my life. In the beginning, after I was coming back to life it was a great feeling and I felt very happy. But as time kept on passing by and I found myself in the routine of the every-day chores, the burden began to also fall upon me.

Even though I was extremely happy and excited about taking care of Hailie, the time did come that it was not always easy for me. I already had been drained by the hard task of having taken care of my mother for three years as she was sick with cancer. Also, I had all this ambitions and goals for my life to achieve, such as becoming a professional psychologist and a career woman, but all that was put on a hold first because I had to take care of my mother, then because I became sick and now because I had to take care of my niece full time.

All these events that stopped me from finishing college and stopped me from working and becoming independent were completely out of my control. After I graduated from high school, I had it all planned out, but it seems that God had different plans for me than the ones I had. And no matter how much I tried, He was going to get His way with me.

For I know the thoughts that I think toward you, saith the Lord, thoughts of peace, and not of evil, to give you an expected end. Jeremiah 29:11

My brother was very young when Hailie arrived in our lives, he was also very wounded by my mother's death, and in my opinion he and my father did not handle her death very well either. But unlike me, they manifested their pain in a whole different manner. My brother was just never home. He was always out working or with his friends hanging out. He would only be home to sleep or to party. Thus, there were many times that I did not really want to be home taking care of Hailie, but I had no choice because her mom moved to GA and my father and brother were out of the house before I could even protest. I cried a lot because I wasn't happy about this new job I had inherit without any saying in the matter. At first it was good because taking care of her got me better, but once I was recovering, I certainly desired to have my career. I dreamed about having my own job and making my own money, but that was not possible. Someone had to be home with Hailie and that someone became me.

However, the pain about how unfair I thought this sometimes felt would bring me to my knees and I would cry out to God deeply. Then, I would shake it off and make the best of it. I would take Hailie out to the Park, read to her the toddlers Bible, teach her gospel songs and play with her as I would also work extremely hard cleaning the house that was insanely dirty sometimes, because my brother would come over with all his friends and leave a total mess for me to clean up. I spent hours and hours washing the dishes by hand, because we didn't have a dish washing machine and I spent many hours doing the laundry and drying the clothes by hanging them toward the sun because the drier was broken for months. I would spend hours cooking for Hailie, feeding her, bathing her, etc… It most certainly did not feel like a vacation or as if I was just chilling doing nothing at home all day. I was right back at my previous job, when I was mom to my own mother and had to do all those things for her.

At night time, I would be able to get my mom's car and drive Hailie to church with me. And for a very long time I took her with me to church at night time, many nights. I had everyone praying for her and most people thought she was my daughter. She used to call me mommy!

This whole process with Hailie was bittersweet and still is. But I know that even though it was very painful for me to do all that hard work and have everyone around me think I was having a vacation of a life because I had other people financially maintaining me while I "stayed home with Hailie," I still know that it was a great work of art from God toward me of transforming my heart. He began the work through the process of my taking care of my mother, but then He continued it through having me take care of Hailie.

What I learned through this experience is pure self-denial. There is no better remedy to self-centeredness, selfishness, greed and narcissism than that of having to take care of someone else without any real financial reward or without much recognition of how much you are actually doing and how valuable what you do really is. Even though they were financially maintaining me, it doesn't feel the same as when we earn our own money and maintain ourselves. There is a sense of pride that comes from doing that, yet "pride" was precisely what God was dealing with me in my life. I didn't realize it then, but I was very prideful, and He was skillfully removing all that evil pride out of my heart, by humbling me into the position of a maid and a nanny that "no one ever needed," yet everyone loved to use!

In conclusion, my liberation wasn't only casting demons out of my life, it wasn't only having to renew the spirit of my mind by reading and studying the Bible, it wasn't only going to church and listening to thousands of sermons, it wasn't only singing for hours and hours and hours to God with all my might, it wasn't only praying without ceasing and fasting and interceding... My liberation was much more than all of that, it was also learning to humble myself and let God do His will on my life. It was also letting other people misjudge me and misjudge my daily activities and intentions and not defend myself, it was also allowing myself to be vulnerable and allow myself to be taken care of by those who sometimes mistreated me and where unfair to me and took my labor for them for granted, so that I can serve them and do the will of my Heavenly Father. My liberation was so much more than just demons coming out of my life through prayer, it was loving Hailie as my own daughter and opening up my heart to her, knowing that she will be ripped away from me whenever her parents felt like it and that there was nothing that I can do to stop them! My liberation came from learning to die to myself and live for God, it came from learning to love others as myself, to love others with all my heart without protecting myself. It came from volunteering into going into the cross and learning to live like Christ!

> **Charity (Love) suffereth long, and is kind; charity (Love) envieth not; charity (Love) vaunteth not itself, is not puffed up, doth not behave itself unseemly, seeketh not her own, is not easily provoked, thinketh no evil; rejoiceth not in iniquity, but rejoiceth in the truth; beareth all things, believeth all things, hopeth all things, endureth all things. Charity (Love) never faileth: but whether there be prophecies, they shall fail; whether there be tongues, they shall cease; whether there be knowledge, it shall vanish away. 1 Corinthians 13:4–8**

> **Then said Jesus unto His disciples, if any man will come after Me, let him deny himself, and take up his cross, and follow Me. Matthew 16:24**

> **But Jesus called them unto Him, and said, suffer little children to come unto me, and forbid them not: for of such is the kingdom of God. Luke 18:16**

CHAPTER 5

LEARNING TO LIVE IN THE SPIRIT AND NOT IN THE FLESH

This I say then, walk in the Spirit, and Ye shall not fulfill the lust of the flesh. For the flesh lusteth against the Spirit, and the Spirit against the flesh: and these are contrary the one to the other: so that ye cannot do the things that ye would. Galatians 5:16–17

Transitioning my life into the spirit was no easy task for me. I was used to a very liberal lifestyle. By the time I was liberated from the legion of demons, I was used to speaking with cuss words, dressing very provocative, listening to secular music, watching whatever I desired to see in TV, I got hooked on smoking cigarettes in the mental institution, because it would calm me down from the anxiety the psychiatric medications gave me and I also was hooked on smoking marijuana. I loved smoking weed! I also drank alcohol, but I don't believe I was an alcoholic, even thou I was able to outdrink many of the toughest male friends I had. I had lived a party animal lifestyle most of my teenage years and the time had come for me to reflect on my actions and genuinely repent!

Becoming a decent child of God was looking like a huge mountain for me to climb. However, the fear and anxiety I had experienced during my whole ordeal in 1996 was enough motivation for me to give it my best shot. I had been so tormented by all those demons that I became one hundred percent determined to change! I was not going to allow those hideous creatures back into my mind to control my life once again. Whatever God desired me to give up, I was determined to give it up. Everything He asked I was going to try my hardest to quit, everything except weed! For some reason, I thought it was impossible for me to quit smoking weed.

Thus, my journey in ridding myself from my sinful habits began. It turned out that quitting smoking cigarettes was much harder than I had imagined it would be. My body experienced major withdraws from the nicotine. I had done everything I could do to quit, but I found myself relapsing over and over again. But quitting smoking cigarettes became much more important than just doing it to try to please God, I was in a point that I could not breath right. I would run out of air sometimes and I had to grab a Vicks vaporizer and inhale the vapor to help me breath better. It was a horrible sensation. I hated it. I hated the way the cigarettes controlled my life. I really wanted to quit. But I could not do it. At least not on my own strength. So after I had done everything in my power to quit and failed, I decided to fast about it. I fasted for twenty-four hours one day of no eating any food or drinking any water throughout the whole time. All I did that day was pray about it and smoke cigarettes while praying. Yes, you read that right, I smoked cigarettes throughout the entire fast that I did to quit smoking cigarettes. Like I said, I could not quit, I needed God to help me. So I wasn't going to wait for me to quit smoking, to then fast about it, because I could not do that, even if I wanted to. But to my surprise it actually worked! Believe it or not, the next day I never smoked a cigarette again, and then again, the next day and the next. After that fast, I never smoked again. It has been more than two decades and I have not touched a single cigarette since then.

Then he answered and spoke unto me saying, This is the word of the Lord unto Ze-rub'ba-bel, saying, Not by might, nor by power, but by My Spirit saith the Lord of hosts. Zechariah 4:6

Is not this the fast that I have chosen? To loose the bands of wickedness, to undo the heavy burdens, and to let the oppressed go free, and that you break every yoke? Isaiah 58:6

The day came where I found myself throwing my provocative clothes away with tears in my eyes. It was extremely painful for me to do that, for I loved my clothes and how they made me feel and look. But I did it! I forced myself to stop listening to secular music and I craved the secular songs I was used to listening to, but I restrained myself from putting them on. Instead, I had the Christian radio on all the time. I stopped watching TV and all those types of things in the media that were wicked and instead, I spent hours and hours studying the Bible and listening to sermons. I tried to stop cussing, but it took a while, because everyone in my life cussed too and it was just extremely hard for me to stop while having to constantly listen to everyone else say a cuss word every other word they spoke. I wrote a bunch of verses on colorful paper and pasted them all over my room and turned my room into a gigantic Bible. The moment I would open my eyes from my bed, I would see the word of the Lord starring back at me. That was how I would wake up every morning. I would read them all out loud daily, and they were a lot. My door and walls were covered with huge verses of the Bible written with black markers.

I was on my way to becoming a real woman of God, but I still smoked weed. I really did not have such a strong conviction that I needed to quit. I used to smoke weed right before going to church and I would be there all high as a kite. I used to study the Bible stoned as well. But the Holy Spirit was patiently working on convicting me that I should quit. As time passed by, I began to feel the conviction that I needed to stop smoking weed as well. I already had stopped drinking alcohol. Alcohol was probably the easiest thing for me to quit.

One day as I was smoking a joint, I prophesied on front of a video camera that my friends were filming, that God was going to remove marijuana out of my life as well. After I declared those words, I took a toke from my joint.

But even though I smoked, I was now convinced that it was time to quit! The time came that I did not like anything controlling my life and I realized that weed had a stronghold on me. I did not like depending on herb to feel happy. I wanted to be free from it all and just depend solely on God, whom seems to have been the One who placed that desire upon my heart. He wanted to be the sole source of my joy, my peace and happiness and He did not want anything in my life taking Him out of that role. But weed did that, it removed Him out of my heart a little bit. It was like an idol, as so many other things that I had been working on quitting. After two years of smoking weed after I received Jesus Christ in my heart in 1996, I decided to quit.

But just as it happened to me with cigarettes, quitting weed was not as easy as I thought it would be. I relapsed a lot! I think fasting wasn't as effective with weed as it was with cigarettes either. So this was what God decided to do to help me quit for good. One day, after I had promised God I would not smoke weed again, a friend came up to me with his joint and offered me a hit. I said no, but then hesitated and said to myself: "Oh, just one more time..." So I left to his car to go smoke with him. As I sat in the car, with the joint in my hand ready to smoke, I watched in absolute horror, my little York Shier dog that I had owned for more than ten years, my dog that I absolutely loved as if she was my child, I watched her run toward the streets looking for me, I saw her going toward the running cars in the street, and I just prayed: "Oh, please God, don't let her get killed!" And I saw how she miraculously was somehow placed on the sidewalk so fast, as if an angel had grabbed her out of the street where the cars drove by and where I saw her go to, and was gently placed right back into the side walk. I screamed out her name really loud and ran to her and grabbed her, hugged her and kissed her with what it seemed to me as if my heart was raising one hundred miles per hours. I was so relieved that she was still alive and safe. The road that she ran toward to was always full of running cars who drive by pretty fast. Thus, right after she was put back into the sidewalk there were several cars that drove by there really fast, so she could have easily been killed that day.

I sat down in the sofa and felt embarrassed with God, because I was about to smoke weed and still, He was kind enough to not let my dog die. That would have devastated me! I thanked Him wholeheartedly and in shame I asked Him to forgive me for almost smoking weed again. Then I clearly heard His voice tell me: "I did not save your dog, just to save her. I wanted to show you that in the same way that she almost ran unto her death, in the same way you do that when you go smoke weed." Those words sunk into my heart deeply and never again did I ever smoke another joint!

There is a way which seems right unto a man, but the end thereof are the ways of death. Proverbs 14:12

Furthermore, during these days my father had hired a nanny for Hailie from Costa Rica, I started a job in a hotel in Miami Beach. This hotel was owned by famous celebrities. I saw them there all the time. I saw other celebrities who liked going there such as Shakira, Mariah Carey, etc. It was a different experience for me working there as a woman of God. I had already had jobs prior to that one, but it was when I was liberal and like most people. Working in a secular job now was much more difficult for me, because I had to try to stay "holy" in the midst of very unholy people. Everyone in the restaurant who worked together with me loved to cuss as they spoke, the music that was on all the time was secular, promoting all those sinful things I had been trying so hard to give up and crucify. People smoked cigarettes right on front of me all the time and they had conversations among each other on front of me about sex, drugs and partying that would stir up my flesh.

It was very hard to stay in the spirit in the midst of all of that. I fasted a lot, while working there. I witnessed to many people in the restaurant. Some of them worked with me in the restaurant, while others worked for the hotel in the housekeeping department. I won many of them for the Lord and prayed for many of them. I even got the whole staff from the restaurant to pray with me before we all ate together prior to the beginning of our shift. There was one guy who would always listen to my words about Christ, he missed work one day and I was burdened in my spirit by his absence. I ended up finding out that he overdosed on drugs and that he was in the hospital in a coma fighting for his life. I decided to go visit him at the hospital after my shift was done. I was able to go to him. He was completely unconscious. He had tubes all over his body and it was truly painful for me to watch him. I opened my Bible and sat down next to him. I read the Bible out loud to him for hours and hours. I must have been there for almost four hours reading when out of nowhere, he woke up! His name was Lazarus. He was Cuban. He woke up out of his comma and starred at me in the face and said: "Desiree, I thought that I was dreaming that you were preaching to me"? I said: "No, you are not dreaming, I am here and is because God loves you. Lazarus, please accept Jesus Christ as your Lord and Savior today so that He can heal you and save you." He replied, "I can't do that because I am gay!" Then I replied, "God doesn't care about that, He wants for you to come as you are and then He will guide your path, He died for you and loves you and doesn't want you to die today" He replied, "Okay." So I led him in prayer to receive the Lord as His Lord and Savior and to ask Him for forgiveness and then after he prayed with me, he laid down and immediately fell back to sleep.

I went back home and the next day I went to work. He showed up but, not to work, he came over to look for me. He told me they had just released him out of the hospital and said that he would make a full recovery and that he decided to come to look for me to ask me to give him a Bible. I said of course, and I gave him my Bible, after he got my Bible, I found out he had no recollection in his memory that I had been in the hospital praying for him the night before. He only had an "urge" to seek God and I was the only one he knew that talked about God. But he had no memory of him praying with me in the hospital. He must have come out of the comma in his spirit by the grace and mercy of God. There is no explanation for his recovery other than the power of the blood of Jesus and the power of prayer and repentance. Hallellujah!

But He was wounded for our transgressions, He was bruised for our iniquities, the chastisement of our peace was upon Him; and with His stripes we are healed. Isaiah 53:5

Sometimes after work, I used to walk toward the ocean and sit down under the moon light and just read the Bible out loud. It was so serene. I enjoyed that so much. One time I remember that after having sat down on front of the ocean, on the sand, I read the Book of Isaiah out loud for hours, then when I got up to go, I was stunned to see that I actually had an audience listening to me reading all of that time without me knowing they were there. It was incredible!

I preached to a lot of people, in the job and in the beach. I even was able to tell Shakira that Jesus loved her as I passed by her in the midst of the people that were gathered around her. She smiled and thanked me.

Unfortunately, the gay community that worked with me in the restaurant was not too happy with me saying God bless you to them. They started complaining about me and eventually I got fired! I was told I was fired from there strictly for preaching. They advised me to work in a nursing home or a place like that. I was deeply hurt. I went home that night and held Hailie in my arms and prayed to God to heal me. I then clearly heard the voice of the Lord say to me: "The hotel did not do injustice against Desiree, but against Jesus Christ, therefore it will fall under a curse." I was startled by that thought and truly did not know what to make of it. Several months later I had to go by to get my paper work for my taxes only to find the restaurant closed down. I ran into one of the housekeepers that I had made friends with and whom received Jesus Christ with me. He was so happy to see me and told me that after they fired me, things in the restaurant completely changed. He said that he believed with all his heart that it had to do with me and them firing me. I was stunned! He said that the first thing that began to happen was that the guests began to complain a lot about the food, then he said that one by one, all the people that had complained about me began to get fired themselves. Then he said that things got so bad that they had to close the restaurant down. I was speechless!

I also heard that the hotel's owner's home in Miami Beach was robbed shortly after I was fired. The restaurant was eventually re-opened again, but it definitely took a long time for them to re-open it. That lesson taught me to always pray for mercy toward those who persecute me. Because they are not messing with me, but with Almighty God Himself!

Dearly beloved, avenge not yourselves, but rather give place unto wrath; for it is written, Vengeance is mine; I will repay, saith the Lord. Romans 12:19

Perhaps, I can understand some people don't want to hear about God while being in their job, but how is it fair for those of us who don't want to hear cuss words, conversations about sex, drugs and partying, secular music that promotes sin or have cigarette smoke on our face and hair all the time, how come is perfectly fine for us to endure all of that while we work?

Why is it that we are not allowed to express our truth, but everyone else is perfectly fine expressing their sin?

He that is not with Me is against Me; and he that gathereth not with Me scattereth abroad. Matthew 12:30

CHAPTER 6

LEARNING TO SERVE THE LORD

And whatsoever ye do, do it heartily, as to the Lord, and not unto men; knowing that of the Lord ye shall receive the reward of the inheritance: for ye serve the Lord Christ. Colossians 4:23–24

Even though I now became unemployed, when we belong to Jesus Christ, we are never unemployed.

Therefore said He unto them, the harvest truly is great, but the labourers are few; pray ye therefore the Lord of the harvest, that he would send forth labourers into his harvest. Luke 10:2

It turned out that I was needed back in the house with Hailie, because unfortunately our nanny was busted in Dadeland Mall shop lifting and shortly after that, she was sent back to Costa Rica. Thus, I took care of Hailie once again full time. I did have some real rough days with her. Aside of many sleepless nights, monitoring her fevers and dealing with her ear infections, she was also acting out and sometimes would behave badly. But I understood her. I knew she probably missed her real mom who was nowhere to be seen and my brother was also always out working and then our home was chaotic with never ending partying. A lot of partying was still going on with my brother and his friends and sometimes my father would go away to Puerto Rico and leave us alone in our house and it was like a club in there. I used to try to take Hailie out of the house as much as possible. But regardless, trying to sleep in the house was very hard for me. The music and people talking would never stop. Hailie learned to fall asleep through the noise, but I could not. But still, I truly believe that all those things caused her anxiety and then she would display that anxiety in the way she would behave. I started having people in my church get annoyed at her and me. They started telling me that I needed to discipline her more and that I was too passive. They wanted me to hit her every so often. But I did not think spanking her was necessary. I thought what she really needed was a lot of attention, love, affection and prayer. However, in my church the leaders did not agree with me at all and they would tell me I was doing it all wrong. It became very painful for me, because they were getting aggressive trying to discipline me for not disciplining Hailie their way. But even though they all thought I was wrong and became brutal with me about it, by the grace of our Lord Jesus Christ and by His wisdom and love and perseverance, I was able to proof all of them wrong to the point that they had to apologize to me in the end.

I did it my way regardless of how much peer pressure they gave me to spank her and it paid off big time. I just had a routine with Hailie. Every day we would play together, sing, pray, read her toddlers Bible which became a blessing to me because I learned the Bible together with her in a very simple and fun way. Teaching her new things brought the best out of me. Whenever she was out of control, I would just put her on time out. Furthermore, I used to make her kneel and pray and ask God to help her to behave better and she would do it. It would have been much easier to just spank her, and I knew that it would be easier, but that would not have worked. I didn't want her to just be obedient out of fear alone, I wanted her to be obedient out of love and for the sake of tranquility and peace within her soul. That is the difference between spanking her and working hard at her healing process. As I worked hard at her healing process, I saw a side of myself that I liked very much, and I chose to keep doing it.

She was getting healed by the whole process, but so was I. She became calm and peaceful and so did I. I prayed my heart out for her to be at peace every day. I would place my hands on her head and anointed her with oil and pray and worship over her, again and again. It was a lot of work, but it paid off! She was a totally different child and the people in my church noticed! The most incredible miracle about all this wasn't her incredible transformation, even though that was a huge deal, but it was that I was able to do this in the middle of pure chaos. My house was insane! I must say that after my liberation, Hailie's transformation was the next most amazing experience for me concerning the power of God. He is amazing! Nothing is impossible for Him!

Sadly, even though Hailie and I got very used to each other, as mother and daughter, all that did not matter, in one day, when she was almost three years old, her mother came back to Miami, picked her up and moved her away to Georgia. And just like that, I was left with this huge void in my heart and I had no idea how to get rid of the pain. I couldn't even visit her because she was out of the state. Oh my…how I cried for my Hailie so bad! It was by far one of the worst feelings of my life. She was not just a niece to me, she really was and still is my real first baby.

But the Lord had new plans for me, and He most certainly knew how to keep me busy. I met this young woman in church, I will name her Karen, but that is not her real name. When we met, she did not like me at all. She confessed this to me later, on our journey together. I guess the enemy knew that God had planned to use me to help her, because help her is what I did. She was in her early twenties. She was addicted to cocaine and other drugs. She was looking for God. But she was very messed up. I moved her in with me, my father was okay with it and allowed me to bring her in. She slept next to me in my bed. I learned liberating people through this experience. This woman was full of demons and they would manifest all the time. I had to be constantly praying and casting her demons out. I took care of her almost the same way I was taking care of Hailie. I would read to her the Bible a lot, I would sing and pray over her with oil, I taught her how to fight the demons and would preach to her all the time. She used to get lost from time to time. She would go to be with her old friends who did drugs and I used to have to go find her. It was a lot of hard work. But she was getting better and so was I. Because we grow in faith and knowledge and wisdom as we help others. Thus, it was a blessing for me to help her out as much as it was a blessing for her to be helped by me.

From time to time, her demons would threaten me through her own mouth and they would call me bad names. But I would not relent. I fought for this woman as if she was me. She would take off from my house from time to time wanting nothing else with me, to then come right back for me to help her again. On one of those times of her been gone, my father came over my room one day to let me know that he was moving to Puerto Rico and that we all had to move because we had lost our home and could no longer afford living there. He asked me to move with him because he did not want me to be alone or by myself. I thought about it. I even had been offered a great job assisting one of my father's friend in Puerto Rico who used to be a film producer. His friend once came over our home and had seen some things that I had written that were very artistic and he had mentioned to my father that he would love to have me work for him in a new film that he was working on. I was actually very excited about that. I thought that finally I was going to get a break from all these vile chores and get to work in things that I truly enjoy. But when I brought all this up to the Lord, I was told that all of that was a trick from Satan to distract me. He told me that it was not the right time for me to work in that field. He said that I was being trained by God in liberation from demons and that was the reason the devil was proposing this opportunity in Puerto Rico. Satan wanted me to stop learning on how to liberate others from demons and to get distracted from learning about God and get me to be busy doing everything else that had nothing to do with what I was doing.

> **Again, the devil taketh Him up into an exceeding high mountain, and sheweth him all the kingdoms of the world, and the glory of them; And saith unto him, all these things will I give thee, if thou wilt fall down and worship me. Then saith Jesus unto him, Get thee hence, Satan: for it is written, thou shalt worship the Lord thy God, and Him only shalt thou serve. Matthew 4:8–10**

So even though it was extremely painful for me to decline the offer for the job in Puerto Rico, I declined it. And even though it took all the courage in the world to choose to separate from my dad and live on my own, I did. I moved into a loft that my father paid for me for the first month and I got me a new job as a telemarketer right across my apartment. Unfortunately, I started getting callers complaining to me about how the package we were selling them were not getting to them, or some sort of missing product. I realized that a lot of the things we were being trained to say to our customers were false and misleading and I decided to leave the job, because lying is a sin.

> **Thou shalt not bear false witness against thy neighbor. Exodus 20:16**

Ye shall not steal, neither deal falsely, neither lie one to another. Leviticus 19:11

A month or so after I left that job, the cops raided the office and so many people got arrested! I had never been so glad to have quit a job than this time. What would have happened to me if I would have still been working there when that raid occurred? Only God knows...

In thee have they taken gifts to shed blood; thou hast taken usury and increase, and thou hast greedily gained of thy neighbours by extortion, and hast forgotten me, saith the Lord God. Behold, therefore I have smitten mine hand at thy dishonest gain which thou hast made, and thy blood which hath been in the midst of thee. Can thine heart endure, or can thine hands be strong, in the days that I shall deal with thee? I the Lord have spoken it and will do it. Ezekiel 22:12–14

Moreover, I went to an employment agency to find a good job, but it was not easy because I did not have a car, because my last car broke down for good before I moved out on my own and I had no money to get a new one. Thus, I relied on public buses which were not too reliable. I also did not have too much knowledge on computers since my college career had been abruptly interrupted by my mother's illness and death. But regardless, even though I did not have too much knowledge on computers I tried to work as a receptionist in an office near my apt. This employment agency would have me work for the company as a temporary employee, if after three months, the company liked me, they would keep me, but if they didn't like me, I would have to go look for a new job. Unfortunately, because of not knowing much about computers I had to find a new job. I then tried a job as a receptionist in a firm in Brickell. This job was much further from me and I had to travel to it in bus and train. But if I could pull it off, it was a very luxurious office and the pay was good, thus I had potential to make a decent living there.

Meanwhile, I was excited that I finally had privacy in the place I lived. I finally had silence. Oh my... How I appreciated Silence!

And even though there were some scary moments for me in that loft, because I was utterly alone, I did not really mind it in comparison to the peace and silence that I was experiencing and had no idea how that felt, ever. And that fear that I had to confront all by myself in that place only made me stronger. However, one day when I went to church, the Pastor gave me a prophesy that changed all that all over again. He prophesied to me that if I lived alone, who will I preach to? Myself in the mirror? This prophesy really shook me to the core, because when the Pastor told me that, he did not know I had a couple of people that God was asking me to move in with me, but I was ignoring Him about it, because I wanted to be alone and take a break from living with others and dealing with drama that seem to linger upon me like a shadow.

But I had to be obedient and with much pain in my heart, I obeyed. I moved Karen again into my loft. One day, her demons were out of control and this time I freaked out within me, because we were all alone. I thought to myself that surely I would die that day if the Lord did not intervene. She almost threw herself down the stairs! I prayed and interceded for her night after night. It was an ongoing battle. But thankfully, the Lord was faithful, and the demons were subjected under His control. She did not have a job and I used to have her reading the Bible at home while I would go to work and then we would go to church every night. Then, I moved in two more friends from church who needed help as well and they also did not have jobs. We all went together to church at night. To say that I was pretty stressed out with so many ladies in my apartment without a job and with demons is an understatement. But the Lord helped me through it.

Aside of practicing delivering others from demons at my home, I also learned much about it in church. I saw hundreds of people get their demons cast away by the leaders, just as it had been done to me. That became a normal sight for me in this church. I learned so much about spiritual warfare. I was trained how to do spiritual warfare by the leaders very well and I also read a book called "He Came To Set The Captives Free" by Rebecca Brown. This book became my guideline on liberation. I read it three times and everyone that I was delivering from demons, I would make sure they would read it.

After a while of helping these girls at my loft/apt, they moved out. I was back alone. But it became so challenging for me to pay my rent. I met a guy in my job at Brickell, whom I really liked. He started offering me rides home after work. He did not know the Lord, but I led him to know him. I took him to my church, and he liked it. He became very interested in the word of God and we would talk about God and the Bible for hours and hours. We ended up falling in love. Even though I thought that we were moving too fast for my comfort zone, the whole rent issue had me troubled. I needed help to pay my place, I really could not afford it alone, so I decided to move him in with me. Our pastor married us and we prayed and asked God to give us a child and we promised God that if He gave us a child, we would raise him or her according to His ways. I didn't think that we should be having a child yet, since I didn't have a car and my financial situation wasn't stable and he did not have much money either, but for some reason he was really wanting a child and I trusted him and I trusted God that if He gave us a child, we would be okay. We were both in our late twenties, so age wise we were ready. Besides, he really seems to love me, so he made me believe.

I must admit, that one day in church, I did sort of get a warning from God about this relationship. A lady with a gift of prophesy, prophesied to me that there was a proposition given unto me that was not the will of God. But I did not heed the warning. Moreover, even though this guy had been on fire for the Lord for the first couple of months, when he saw how faithful I was in giving the church my tithes and when he saw that we didn't have much money left after the tithes, well that bothered him a lot. But I was always very faithful with my tithes and took great joy in giving them. It was an honor for me to pay my tithes and still is. I knew that blessings do happen when we give, whether it is through tithings and offerings or charities. Not only do I tithe because I get blessed in return, I tithe because it gives me a great sense of purpose in my life. And is not as if I always had a check from a formal job that I was able to pay my tithes from. Thus, I was not going to stop tithing no matter what. I had made many vows to God after my liberation that I was going to obey Him no matter the cost, and I meant it!

Unfortunately, I did not pass my trial period at the job in Brickell. I bumped into the same situation as the previous job, they needed someone with more computer knowledge. Thus, I got a different job that wasn't a receptionist. I got hired as a front desk clerk in a nice hotel near my house.

My experience at the hotel was bittersweet. At first, it was very hard. Every job is never pleasant at the beginning. That whole training period can be very painful. Not knowing anything and having to remember so much information at once can be very scary. But even though that is the main problem with every first time at a job, my problem became another thing. Aside from the trauma of having left three different jobs back to back and still having to figure out how to pay my rent in the midst of that mess, in the hotel, the front desk staff was all trained into lying to their guests. Yes, you read that right. Let me explain: When they book the rooms, the sales staff for the booking department, they are all trained to overselling four to five extra rooms. This is a strategy that they use to ensure that if anyone canceled their reservation, they would still have all the rooms sold.

Furthermore, most certainly there are people who cancel their reservations at the last minute, but there are those occasions when everyone who made a reservation shows up and then the front desk staff must face the few extra people who reserved rooms which are occupied. So to these people who come to the hotel very tired from their trip into the hotel, ready to shower and go to sleep, the front desk staff must inform them that they have no room available even though they made their reservation. They then move on and say this huge lie about how the guest that was there prior to them had an emergency and had to stay longer or some other crazy lie like that. They then have them leave the hotel and go to another one. Thus, when they were training me to tell the guest that lie, to look at them in the eye and just plain simply lie to their face, I refused!

Not only is that very unethical, is very rude! Also, I hate it when people lie to me, thus, how dare I lie to others and then expect others to not lie to me as well?

**Be not deceived; God is not mocked;
for whatsoever a man soweth, that shall
he also reap. Galatians 6:7**

Hence, there were some guests that were not dumb and didn't fall for the lie and would tell off the clerk who dared to lie to them. They would get very angry. But all of that wasn't the only reason why I refused to lie, although they were good reasons. I was liberating people from demons. I knew that sin gives them place and that they get major authority against me and my loved ones through any sin in my life. I could not afford to lie to anyone about anything.

That is a very dangerous thing to do if you are going to be liberating others from demons. I also didn't have any intentions to let the demons that were cast out of me to come back. The Bible says that if we continue to practice sin, purposely, those demons come back in us seven times stronger.

When the unclean spirit is gone out of a man, he walketh through dry places, seeking rest, and findeth none. Then he saith, I will return into my house from whence I came out; and when he is come, he findeth it empty, swept, and garnished. Then goeth he, and taketh with himself seven other spirits more wicked than himself, and they enter in and dwell there; and the last state of that man is worse than the first. Even so shall it be also unto this wicked generation. Matthew 12:43–45

Neither give place to the devil. Ephesians 4:27

When I told my trainer that I was not going to lie to the guest, all hell broke loose against me. They called their supervisor and the one above them and one by one, I told them all that I was not going to lie. They could not understand why, so I told them that I was a Christian and that Christians are not supposed to lie. They told me that there were many Christians working there and that they all lied.

But I insisted that I was not going to do that. I was able to see their anger toward me. They placed me in an office and spoke very seriously to me. By now, I had already been well trained in almost everything. They already had invested a lot on me, and I had already endured enough pain and agony to not wish to start a different new job to have to relearn everything again. But I was determined to do what was right and holy. No matter the cost!

When they saw that I was dead serious and that I was not going to budge no matter what, they threatened to fire me. They told me to go home and think about my decision and to come back the next day with my answer. But they left the firing me part on the table for me to know that if I chose to not lie, I may not have a job.

When I got home that night I was in great agony. That whole process had been very painful and scary. I didn't want to go back, but the Lord told me to go back and give them my answer, so I did. When they heard that I would not do it, they were infuriated with me and I was sure that I was going to be fired. My legs were trembling, and my hands were sweating, I had weird butterflies in my stomach and I really had to pray hard within me to not faint, but to my surprise they did not fire me.

Instead, they put me back in the front desk and began a war against me. They all joined forces together to make me want to quit. I was getting written up a lot for the stupidest things, they were trying to make me fail in whatever I did. I assume it was illegal for them to fire me for not lying so now they had to figure out a way to get rid of me without them looking bad. It was so hard for me. I was being tortured. I would get home and cry my heart out night after night. I was going to work trembling just thinking about what kind of trouble was I going to be in next. It became so stressful and painful that I became forgetful and to add injury to my wound, I began making silly mistakes and forgetting details that were very important. By now I wanted to quit for real, I didn't care to look for a different job and relearn all over again the next job, I just wanted the torture to end. But when I would pray to the Lord about it, He kept on prohibiting me from quitting the job and told me to keep going. It lasted for long, painful months.

They must have been shocked at my coming back and not quitting, because honestly, any normal human being would have quit long time ago. They could not fire me, I would not quit, so the next step for them was to remove me out of the front desk. Well, there was a young lady that had been working in a position in the hotel called: "Quality Control Ambassador." This was a job outside of the front desk. She had her own office and she was above the managers and front desk staff. She was working all day long on her own. No one was really supervising her work throughout the day. Her role was to compensate the guest who had a bad stay. She had to figure out what was the problem, who was at fault and she then had to deal with the managers of the departments that were in fault for the mistake or mishap. She was getting paid much better than the front desk clerks.

Well, this young lady was going to get married and she was going to travel to Colombia and be away for a long time. Thus, even though there were many front desk clerks that had been desiring to have that position, that had been working much longer in the hotel than me and that were sure they would get it before me, well they all got to see me get promoted just like that!

Thou preparest a table before me in the presence of mine enemies: thou anointest my head with oil; my cup runneth over. Psalm 23:5

What an amazing experience that was! I was blown away! My God is great! I loved this job! I did very well too. I always work much better when no one is behind me criticizing my every move, watching over me just to see when they get the chance to rebuke me and correct me and telling me how to do things. I excelled so much here. I met many of the managers of the hotel and one day one of them heard my name and said: "You are Desiree?" He seemed very stunned by my name and I said yes, then he said: "Oh, you have no idea! We would have meetings about you. We all heard that you would not lie, and we were all very impressed by your faith. They did not know what to do concerning you!" He smiled at me and shook my hand and told me it was an honor to meet me. He was a Christian too. I was speechless!

Moreover, I met many guests and really enjoyed compensating their stay and making them smile and I also met many of the housekeepers and other staff members and of course I preached to many of them and led them to the Lord. I was so happy in this job, but unfortunately 9/11/01 happened and when those twin towers tumbled down, they tumbled down the best job I had so far. After 9/11 in 2001 happened, people did not want to travel that much anymore, and the hotel industry took a huge blow. Many people had to be laid off from the hotel and I was one of them. It was a very sad time for me. I saw many old people that had been working at the hotel for decades lose their job. My heart broke for those people.

Once again, I found myself struggling to pay the rent and the light bill. The government helped us and paid checks to people like me, that were laid off because of 911 and that helped me get by during those next months. My sister also sent me some money from New York where she lived with her boyfriend. However, my financial struggle was dire and real! I was starting to feel worn out!

I got a new job at the Parking Violation Bureau in Downtown Miami as I also found out I was pregnant. I would get up every morning and take the bus and the train, I worked on the phones dealing with very angry people who would tell me their complaints about our system of doing things, one example was a caller who claimed that his meter still had time for them to be parked where they were, but still they had a ticket? I did not know how to help those people, because we had no solution other than to charge them the ticket and take their money. If they wanted to dispute the ticket, they had to go to court and go on a mission to resolve something that may not even work for them. It was very discouraging for me to find myself not being able to provide justice for my callers. One more time, I learned how corrupted the workplace is in America. My job here was to charge people's credit cards and collect their parking debt, whether it was fair or not.

By this time, my son's father was not so into church or God anymore. The last prophesy our Pastor gave us together was that trials were about to start to happen in our lives, but that if he kept his eyes on Jesus, he would always have the victory. Unfortunately, as the trials began, he started to look for God less and less. Things in the church were also going bad. Unfortunately, the devil was able to divide the church and close it down. The Pastors ended in divorce and I witnessed many of the congregants fall in a big spiritual mess. Sadly, my best friend from that church committed suicide by hanging herself shortly after. She suffered from bipolar disorder and unlike me, she was not liberated from demons, because she was very intellectual and did not really believe in demons, even though she knew my testimony. She came from a very wealthy family and had been raised in the best schools and was been treated by the best medical doctors who were constantly medicating her with their psychiatric drugs and indoctrinating her about how their way was the only way to healing. I was devastated by her death and heartbroken by the fact that before she died, she had been frantically looking for me to help her; but I was nowhere to be found, because I would purposely stay without phones so that I can keep my own sanity, since I was busy trying to survive my financial situation and I had to hide from people who wanted for me to pray for them, because I was consumed by work and stress!

In my opinion, the biggest mistake I believe the Pastor made was that he was too busy with the ministry and neglected his marriage and family. This is the most common mistake most ministers make. It really takes hard work to make a marriage work and time is of the essence. If you spend all your time working and your spouse and child has no time with you or very little, it is not going to end good. That is common sense!

This defeat upon this ministry was a great blow to my heart. I loved the Pastors and the people of the church like my family and never in a million years would have I ever imagined that the devil would be able to destroy them the way he did. But he did and is not because he is stronger than God, it was because the people gave the devil place.

CHAPTER 7

MY NEW CHURCH

Unfortunately, my son's father had to witness the mess the devil did in the church where I was liberated and as a baby in Christ, I believe that this was devastating for his spiritual growth. He became extremely cautious concerning church and the whole financial situation with us was wearing him out too. He wanted me to stop paying my tithes and I wasn't going to do that, so that became a huge mountain between us. I didn't care that my church had failed, I wasn't going to stop being obedient to God because other people failed. I was determined to start over in a new church and continue to obey. I had gotten saved in 1996 in a church called "El Redentor" which means "The Redeemer." I was there for two years and this was the place where God prepared me spiritually to be able to be liberated. Then I was in the church where I was liberated for four years. This church was called "El Poder Del Evangelio" which means: "The Power of the Gospel." Now God led me to go into a new ministry in Miami called "Ministerio Internacional El Rey Jesus," which means: "King Jesus International Ministries."

Unlike my past two churches, this one was huge. It had thousands of members and the building was big. I was amazed by everything in here. It was very exciting for me. I saw that they knew about liberation and practiced it too, which was not so common for churches to practice. I also saw that they had a powerful intercession and prayer meeting. I once went to one of their service with my son's father whom was extremely skeptical. He had mentioned to me how he thought those people who would fall down on the floor after someone prayed for them were all faking it. Because of what had happened in my past church, he now was skeptical about everything in church. Well, seems as God sure does have a sense of humor, because he got convicted to go up to the altar and allow someone to pray for him and to my surprise, I got to see his feet come up and his head go down on the floor just as he was claiming that those who fell were faking it. I waited for him to get back up, since I did not fall after they prayed for me and was just stunned and curious about what had just happened to him. He was speechless!

For the preaching of the cross is to them that perish foolishness; but unto us which are saved it is the power of God. For it is written, I will destroy the wisdom of the wise, and will bring to nothing the understanding of the prudent. 1 Corinthians 1:18–19

I fell in love with this church. Everything was just exciting and excellent. The people were nice and so organized. The anointing felt powerful and the pastors seemed smart and their sermons were very enlightening to me. However, I did miss my old Pastor's sermons, and to this day, I have never heard anyone preach the gospel with the same boldness my old Pastor had and with so many verses of the Bible. He did not like to speak much of his own words, almost the entire messages were all the word of God and few of his own words. That I missed the most.

During my pregnancy I would wake up early and take a bus and a train to work every day of the week and come back home like at 6:00 or 7:00 p.m. I would cook a meal and eat and then take a bus to church almost every week night as well. I was hungry for God and I could not get enough of him. I was also pregnant and the thought of having a child brought me to my knees more than anything else. I was about to become responsible for another human being and I needed God more than ever because of it. I was also fighting for my relationship with my son's father, since I saw he was going astray from God and no longer wished to come with me to church. He and I spent very little time together because we were always working, and I was in church while he worked. I was really worried about my son's father and I began to go to the prayer meetings that the church had every weekday morning from 5:00 a.m. to 7:00 a.m.

And in the morning, rising up a great while before day, he went out, and departed into a solitary place, and there prayed. Mark 1:35

My voice shalt thou hear in the morning, O Lord; in the morning will I direct my prayer unto thee and will look up. Psalm 5:3

I met people in the church who were kind enough to come to my house and pick me up for those meetings. I believe I was greatly strengthened in my spirit by God through those meetings. But it was a huge sacrifice for me to wake up that early, while being pregnant and having to go to work in public buses and train, after those meetings, to then go back to the services at night time in bus and go to sleep late at night. I slept very little during these days. I was exhausted!

In addition, I had been feeling quite lonely without my mother, my niece, my father, my brother and my sister. All I had left was my little York Shier dog. My worst nightmare had come true, all my most precious people of my life were gone! My mom passed away, my father and brother lived in Puerto Rico, my niece was in Georgia and my sister was living in New York with her boyfriend and I would call her and ask her to move back to Miami because I wanted us to be near each other. But she would tell me that she and her boyfriend were extremely happy in New York, they liked their jobs and lifestyle and they had no desire or intention to move back to Miami. After we would hang up, I used to pray and prophesy that she would come back to Miami in the name of Jesus. Even though she really made me feel that it was never going to happen, I didn't care. I wanted my sister near me, and I prayed hard that she would move back to Miami. After months of exercising my faith and praying without ceasing, I witnessed once again that nothing is impossible for God and that my strongest weapon in this world was prayer. My sister and her boyfriend moved back to Florida, not Miami, but a little bit further. They were close enough for us to drive to each other's place. I was blown away!

But Jesus beheld them, and said unto them, with men this is impossible; but with God all things are possible. Matthew 19:26

Furthermore, during my fourth month of pregnancy, one night I had a very strange feeling concerning my dad who lived in Puerto Rico. The last time I had seen him was a couple of weeks before this night at my sister's new place. He had come to visit us and to see my belly. We had a nice time together and it was quite a family reunion, I did not speak to him for a couple of weeks after that, but I just had a very strong feeling in my intuition that something was wrong with my father. I went to church on that morning and asked the entire group to please pray for my father and they did. When I got back to my place, I heard my phone ringing which was extremely rare since it was 7:00 a.m. and no one really called me at that time. It was my sister letting me know that we had to travel to Puerto Rico because my father was very ill. We went to Puerto Rico that same afternoon and when I got to my uncle's house, he told me that my father had passed away. I will never forget that moment. I was sitting down on his sofa with my belly showing and with my heart waxing within me. I remembered a prophecy someone in my past church had once given me.

Thus, says the Lord: "I am dealing with your bitterness and sadness. I know you have gone through many things and that your past hurts you deeply, but I want you to learn to worship Me in the midst of your pain and agony and you will see how I will pour out supernatural joy and peace that overcomes your pain. Open your mouth and praise and worship Me!"

Then he said unto them, go your way, eat the fat, and drink the sweet, and send portions unto them for whom nothing is prepared: for this day is holy unto our Lord: neither be ye sorry; for the joy of the Lord is your strength. Nehemiah 8:10

After I remembered that prophecy, I thought to myself: "My mother already passed away and all I have left is my dad, but today he passed away too; if I don't sing to God, I will surely die of sadness today." Thus, I opened my mouth and began to worship God. I sang a song in Spanish that is beautiful from Marcos Witt and is a song that gives thanks to God, repeatedly. As I dared to look insane on front of everyone in my uncle's house, I found myself singing this song and as I pressed on singing, I felt this incredible peace that to this day, I have never felt to the extent of how I felt it that day. It was as if I had gotten injected with anesthesia. The pain that I had was fading away and the peace and joy inside my heart is unexplainable. My brother came over to me as I sang and as he was weeping, he threw himself on my lap and began to weep even harder. I didn't stop singing. I just placed my hands on his head and stroked his hair with my fingers and also placed my hand on his back consoling him as I continued to sing as if I was possessed by the Holy Spirit. I could not tell you how long we were there, but it felt as if we were there for a long time.

The next day my brother told someone in the family that when he fell on my lap that day, he experienced a peace upon him that he had never felt before. I already considered myself a radical worshiper because I loved to worship the Lord for many, many hours, but after this experience, I took worship and praise to a totally different level.

When I got back to Miami, things were not getting any better between my son's father and me. I noticed that he was just no longer interested in God or me. He was very distant and indifferent. I tried everything I could to change that, but it was only getting worse by the day. I felt so rejected by him. It was so terrible for me because I was really in love with him. I was also really in need of his emotional support since my father passed away and I was pregnant, but I ended up having to tough all that out by myself. I do thank God for His Spirit and for the many beautiful people in the church that were there for me. They would encourage me with the word of God and pray for me and they even made a surprise baby shower for me, that I almost missed because of how depressed I was that day and almost did not attend the marriage meetings that I had been attending. They spent a lot of money on things for my baby and I could not be more grateful. My lovely sister also threw me a baby shower and I received many things for my son there as well. I was still working and praying and paying my tithes and I was seen the blessings from that.

On my seventh month of pregnancy, my son's father confessed to me that he no longer loved me. I was devastated! He mentioned that he planned on moving out after our son would be born. I told him that if he planned on leaving me, then he should leave now so that I can get used to his absence and prepare myself psychologically to be a single mom. I told him that it seemed to me that it would be much harder to have a new born to attend to, while at the same time dealing with him being away. I thought that if he left now, it would give me time to get used to having him away, so by the time the baby came I was over him, or at least not so devastated. I was suffering a lot anyways by living together with him, but feeling his rejection daily. It was killing me!

Thus, he moved out when I was seven months pregnant. I truly don't know how I did not die of sadness. I couldn't be any more heartbroken. I don't know how I was able to go to work and church and keep doing all the things that I was doing without a car. But by the grace of God, and with many, many tears, I worked almost my entire pregnancy and went to church many nights and mornings.

When my father and my mother forsake me, then the Lord will take me up. Psalm 27:10

A month before my due date, I was way too big to continue to do it all. I was sleeping very little and my body was way too exhausted. I had to make a decision. It was either going to work for my last month of my pregnancy and quit going to church or quit my job and continue to go to church, but I could not do both things.

After much praying and thinking about it, I made my decision, even though I had no idea how I would pay my rent, I chose to quit my job and continue to go to church. The thought of quitting church and praying in the midst of my pregnancy and depression, scared me more than the thought of not having money for my rent. Besides, I had faith and dared to believe that God would provide somehow.

After nine months of being pregnant, the day finally arrived! In the early morning hours my water broke, and my little dog was the only one there to see it. I called my son's father and he came to pick me up and drove me to the hospital. After hours of painful pushing without any epidural, I gave birth to my son and didn't die from the pain as I could have sworn, I would do.

When I was leaving the hospital holding my beautiful newborn in my arms, I clearly heard the Spirit of God say to me: "Take good care of him!" At that moment, those simple words seemed not so challenging, but, boy, oh boy, little did I know the deepness of that statement.

Lo, children are an heritage of the Lord and the fruit of the womb is his reward. As arrows are in the hand of a mighty man; so are children of the youth. Happy is the man that hath his quiver full of them; they shall not be ashamed, but they shall speak with the enemies in the gate. Psalm 127:3–5

My lovely sister slept over my place for the first couple of days after I gave birth and it was a huge help. I was so fragile physically and emotionally. I don't think I have ever been as vulnerable and fragile as I was during those days. After my sister left, I was on my own. Just me, my beautiful little companion/dog and my new baby. There really was no time for me to enjoy the brand-new family member. I had my rent way over due and needed to get right back to work. I didn't know how I was going to pay my rent. I also didn't know how I was going to go back to work since I had no car and taking my son to any daycare without a reliable car was a monumental challenge.

I was overwhelmed by stress. Thankfully, on a morning prayer meeting, the Lord moved mightily on my behalf. I had not said anything about my situation to the people there, and out of nowhere, as I was holding my son in my arms and just praying as we usually did, the leader of the group called me out and asked me to sit in the middle of the whole group. Then he began to speak very nicely about me. Telling everyone how I was a great example of a woman of God and how he had seen me coming to church on bus every day, during my entire pregnancy. He then went on saying that he felt very strongly from God to collect an offering for me and he apologized to me saying he did not mean to offend me in any way or embarrass me, but that he knew God wanted him to do this. To my amazement, they gave me all the money I needed to pay the rent I owed. They saved my apt! God saved my apt through them, hallelujah!

I was so moved by this, I cried so much out of pure joy and relief. I could not believe that had just happened! What a miracle that was indeed!

Moreover, I had to decide concerning my job. I decided to quit the Parking Violation job because it was too far, and I now had to drive my son somewhere for me to be able to work anywhere and without a car that was impossible. I then looked for a job at home and prayed my heart out to find one. And once again, God came through for me. I found a telemarketing job that I can do from my own home. I began working at home on the phones for an insurance salesman. I was his appointment setter. I had to call people from leads that he would give me and convince them to allow him to go over to their house and give them his presentation on his insurance package. I didn't have to sell anything. I only had to convince them to give the man a chance to show them his product and see if they liked to purchase it afterward.

I worked every day of the week from 9:00 a.m. to 9:00 p.m. Sundays were my only day off. I slept very little during the first year of my son's arrival. While I was on the phone all day long with my clients, I had to also breastfeed my son and clean up the house, cook for myself and take care of my son. At night time, I would barely sleep because since I was alone with my son, I was scared he might need something, and I would not wake up to serve him. He would also eat throughout the night time a lot since I was breast feeding him.

I did a lot of worshipping while I breast fed him during the nights. I also went to church every Sunday on bus with my baby. But I had to slow down during the weekdays, because I had to work at night. Thus, I did stop assisting the weeknight services for this period. During my pregnancy I had gained a lot of weight, so now I was also on a mission trying to lose it. Thus, I would do squads while my baby was strapped unto my chest and I was on my telemarketing calls, while doing my squads. That image of me trying to do it all at once is the feminist movement in a nutshell! At first, it might seem heroic, but in truth, this is how women get burned out and children eventually get our leftover energy and devotion! Nothing heroic about that, in my opinion! But sadly, many women such as my-self just simply had no other option, other than to abuse our bodies and minds and give our children our left-over strength and service.

Doing the laundry and groceries became a true challenge for me. The laundry room was downstairs from my apt which only had stairs and no elevators, and I had to take my son with me to do it and wait for it to be done. Luckily, I lived right across a Publix Supermarket, but still I had to take my son in his stroller with me and do a little bit of groceries at a time and walk home with my son and the bags.

What takes someone with a car one hour to do, would take me an entire four to six hours or even more. This is the real struggles of a poor person. One day I experienced one of the most stunning miracles of my life. This elderly man who lived near my apt and whom I had never spoken with, came and knocked on my door; when I opened the door, he was standing there with lots and lots of grocery bags. I looked at him dazed and confused and he just said: "I felt to buy you this, please take them!" I could not believe it! It was probably like $300 worth of food. He must have noticed my struggles, since he must have seen me walking with my baby in his stroller and taking groceries home on foot or taking the bus to go to places. I was a bit embarrassed by the whole event, the same way I felt when the people in the church gave me money, but I was in so much need that I had to learn to receive what others gave me. My pride was being crucified to the max!

Pure religion and undefiled before God and the Father is this, to visit the fatherless and widows in their affliction, and to keep himself unspotted from the world. James 1:27

Meanwhile my son's father was helping me with money very little and sometimes nothing. He would randomly give me money here and there. But I was as broke as can be. My job was paying me salary, but I was making only enough for my rent and my light. I survived with food stamps and with the gifts that those who were kind enough to give me would give me. However, I ate very poorly sometimes and even though I was struggling, I refused to stop paying my tithes. I was determined to obey God in this area, because I felt obeying in this area was going to put an end to my poverty someday and I also saw that paying my tithes was transforming me from the inside. It was forcing me to practice self-denial in a way I had never done before and I saw the changes that were happening within me as a result, changes for the better. This exercise was stripping my pride, my selfishness and greed better than anything else I had ever experienced.

For the love of money is the root of all evil; which while some coveted after,

they have erred from the faith, and pierced themselves through with many sorrows. 1 Timothy 6:10

I really believe that paying our tithes and offerings is the path to prosperity, to learning how to die to ourselves, to bearing real fruits of the Spirit and to learning to depend on God and not on our own strength or money.

Furthermore, as if my life wasn't challenging enough for me, life handed me a curve ball that I had not seen coming. My brother had moved back to Miami after my father died. He had first stayed with me in my apt, but he then moved to an apartment close to mine. My niece ended up having to move back to Miami because her mother had gotten into some type of trouble. But my brother worked as a server in a restaurant and his schedule was nothing like the one Hailie had. She had lived with him for a couple of weeks, but she was not well cared for because of my brother's work schedule and I decided that it was better that she came with me. Sadly, I ended up giving my brother my little dog cause walking and taking care of my dog became a problem for me, because of the baby.

Hailie was five years old. My son was only a few months old and here I was not having any time to grief my only companion who consoled me through my trials, my little dog who was fifteen years old and had been with me since she was a puppy. By now it seemed to me that I was becoming numb. It broke my heart to give her up, but I had no choice! I had too much on my plate. I had to take care of all of us and I was truly on my own. Hailie's dad was not able to give me child support, because his child support money was being deducted out of his paychecks and going straight to her mom in GA. It didn't matter that Hailie was with me and that I was the one that now needed that money. Since she wasn't legally with me, the courts had already arranged that the money go to the mom. I was not able to get any food stamps for her either for the same reason. So I had to share the little bit of money that I was making with her as if she was my child and my responsibility. My brother continued to pay her school bus fare and he had medical insurance for her, but as for everything else, I was on my own.

Taking care of her, after she would be away with her mom was always a great challenge for me. She always came back behaving bad, with lots of anxiety and emotionally unbalanced. She would have outbursts of rage on front of my newborn and sometimes while I was on the phone with my clients. I ended up paying a daycare service right in my neighborhood, $100 a week, just so that I can have an extra hour of peace and quite after school, so that I can work. I was extremely worried on how I would pull this out of taking care of her, because I no longer was all alone or had all the time in the world to focus on fixing her. I was very worried she would traumatize my son with her crying and screaming all the time or that she would cause him to behave bad because of the anxiety she was bringing upon the home. I was so stressed out that my face would have acne break outs like never before. I looked horrible!

Now when I did the laundry it was more than usual, and I had to take two kids with me, instead of one. I also had to go with Hailie and my son on foot to get the groceries. Food ran out quicker and I took longer washing the dishes. We took the bus to church and walked many long miles, I had to put Hailie in the stroller together with my son and push both kids sometimes, because she would get too tired. We used to go walking under the real hot sun and sometimes during the rain. It was extremely tough for all of us. I cried a river! Hailie cried a lot too!

After working for an entire year for the insurance agent, I decided to venture on a different job at home that offered more money. I was desperate for a car and working for the insurance agent was not going to get me the car. I got offered to work as a loan officer from home and I had the potential to earn lots of more money. The only catch to this job was that it was based only on commission. If my boss would not be able to close any business loans from the people that I would provide her by qualifying them, I would not get paid. My boss told me that many of her employees were making lots of money and that if I can get an estimate of fifteen to twenty potential clients in a month, she said that my odds of closing at least one loan were extremely high. If I close only one loan, I would be able to pay my rent for a couple of months at once. I knew how to work hard, I was very used to it by now.

I had done well with my previous job and my last boss was very impressed with my phone skills, he told me that not many people can do that job as efficiently as I had done it. He was very sad when I quit but, he knew I needed more money. I chose to try the loan officer job, because I could not bear my poverty any longer. I started calling the leads just as I did with my previous jobs and I would prequalify many people. I worked from 9:00 a.m. to 9:00 p.m. just as I worked in my previous job. I was so sure I would do well in this job. I had done well in the previous one and it was sort of the same pattern of way of doing things.

Unfortunately, it didn't go well for me. Even though I did my part and gave my boss plenty of prequalified people, she never got to close any business loans with any of them and after two months of working for them, even though my church paid two rents for me to not be evicted, I still got evicted! I was utterly shattered into pieces. I had worked so hard! For nothing. Even though I worked hard, and I had faith, I found myself homeless. All my boss said to me was: "After working in this job for over two decades, I have never seen anyone get so many qualified clients and not have any of them close a deal!" She felt very bad for me, because she knew that I worked super hard and it was out of my hands to close the deals. She was the one who had to close the deals, not me. But it happened! I now had to figure out where I was going to live because I was evicted!

Many are the afflictions of the righteous; but the Lord delivereth him out of them all. Psalms 35:19

CHAPTER 8

MOVING FROM PLACE TO PLACE

A very dear friend of mine from my teenage years, who also happened to assist the same church I was in, offered me to stay with her. She was a single mom too and she had four children. Sadly, once again, after I had already worked very hard to stabilize Hailie, I had no choice but to give her back to her father. The pain in my heart was unbearable! My friend had a two-bedroom apt. and I slept in her children's bunk bed with my son and some of her kids slept in her room. I was so sad during these days. My shame about my financial situation became like a billboard for everyone to see. To add injury upon my wound, many people were gossiping about me, thinking that I had gotten evicted because I didn't work and was just home doing nothing. They were also gossiping among themselves saying that I was crazy and mentally ill and that was what was causing my poverty and my job instability!

As if my life could not get any harder, I had terrible first days in my friend's home. She had gone away for a weekend for a church event and all the kids left too and I stayed all alone with my son for that weekend. My son got very sick and he had a fever. I tried everything I knew to try to lower the fever and prayed all night long to God for healing. But the most terrifying night of my life happened to me in there. My son had a feveral seizure. I watched in pure horror his eyes rolling back and his tiny body jerking back and forth violently. I did not know what to do. My heart sunk deep and time felt as if it stood still. I don't know what was scarier to me, whether my son or the fact that I was all alone with him and with no car. I called 911 and on our way to the hospital we went! They checked him and thankfully he was okay and would recover. They asked me if there was any history in my family of seizures and sure enough, my father, my brother, my nephews and nieces all suffered from seizures as young children. Thus, they said sometimes even if we do everything in our power to lower the fever, it can happen and especially to children who have a family history of it.

This became one more generational curse to pray against.

When my son's father left me, I remember I felt as if I was punished. I didn't understand how this could happen to me. I trusted him. He told me he loved me. He even had a nervous breakdown that ended with him in a hospital, because we had gotten into a dispute and I had decided to leave him. He came back to me begging me to take him back and promising me the world, telling me how he just knew that I was his woman. He had been the one who really desired having a baby during our situation. I was the one that wasn't so sure, but because of his enthusiasm and love for me, I chose to do it. We had prayed for our son before

I got pregnant. My son wasn't an accident! We planned to have him, we asked God to please, please, grant us a child and we even made a vow on front of God and each other that we would raise him according to His holy ways. I feel that I fell in love with my son's father most of all because of the passion and love that I saw he had for God. I loved the way he prayed and listened to His words. I remember he even heard the voice of the Spirit a couple of times. I was sure that if we both loved God and followed Him, we would be okay. But here I am, in a home that was not mine, without a car, without my parents, without a husband or job and with a child that just suffered a seizure and I was the only one in the room to experience it with him...

Being a single mother is a nightmare! I never imagined in a million years that I would be a single mother. I never meant to bring a human being to this earth to be without his father. Yet somehow, I noticed that society doesn't really care that I never chose to separate from the father, they do not care that he was the one who took off and just like that left me alone to fend for myself and my son. Somehow, in this crazy world, if you are poor is because you are lazy and mentally ill and if you are single is because you deserve to be alone. Even though people do help you and you do see some rays of compassion in the middle of dense darkness, truth is that the majority of people only point fingers at you and blame you for your circumstances. The stigma of it all was now heavily hovering upon me, yet I had no time to feel sorry for myself. I had to be strong for my son who depended on me. I had to press forward even though I really wanted to die. I had to keep fighting and trying my best, even though my heart was broken in a million tiny pieces.

Moreover, my friend had what I like to call the "hidden secret weapon": HER MOTHER! Her beautiful mother was a woman of God as well. I will never forget the first day I got there. She saw me and sat me down and told me about a vision the Lord gave her concerning my life. She had been praying about me and my situation and this was what she says the Lord showed her in a vision: "She said she saw me wearing really torn out clothes and that I was walking barefooted. She said I looked dirty and that I was tired. I was walking holding my baby in my arms and as I was walking in what seemed to be a field, I was falling down and scraping my knees and my legs were bleeding. She said she saw me lick my hand and clean my wounds as I would get back up and kept on moving forward. She said I looked so sad and that she actually asked the Lord to stop showing her this vision, because it was too painful for her to watch, but that the Lord insisted that she watches the entire thing.

Then she said she saw me going inside turbulent and dark waters. She saw much algae and I was having to swim through it. I was swimming as I held my child in my arms and the waters were wild. I was swimming in the middle of some things that are placed in the ocean so that people do not cross over. She said that I was swimming in the middle of these things as if that was a path that I was supposed to take. Then she said that after I finished swimming and struggling with my son in the waters, I arrived at my destination and when I got out of the water, Jesus was waiting for me. He then reached out His hand and grabbed my hand and He led me toward a beautiful river. We were walking in a place that seemed to be paradise with really green grass and trees and then the river. This river was beautiful. The waters were crystal clear, and she said that it seemed that it was made from diamonds. Then she said that Jesus told me: "Desiree, these are your tears!" Everything that you went through will be used to bring many souls to My kingdom. Then she saw Him hugging me as I wept in His arms and that was the end of her vision.

She then said that she knew that even though to everyone my life seemed to be a mess, that vision showed her that I was exactly in the perfect will of God and that even though I was experiencing much struggle, poverty and pain, I must keep going forward for His glory. The emotion and sadness that I felt as I heard that woman speak to me all those things is unexplainable. But even though her words pierced my heart like a sharp knife and inflicted much pain, they also encouraged me greatly to keep going.

Her mother used to care for her four children while she looked for work or when she worked. "Oh, if only I had one of those," I thought. Most people take their mothers for granted and don't really understand how much they truly help. Well, her mom offered me to care for my son while I go look for work. My son was one-year-old by now and with my heart melting away within me, I had to leave him with her and go on bus to look for a job where I can get to in time and get out of it in time to get my son out of a daycare, which would be the ultimate goal, since I was not going to leave with my son with my friend's mom for too long, because she really didn't want to have to take care of one more kid. She was already majorly overwhelmed with her four grandchildren, plus a little girl that she had of her own. Her goal was to place all of the children in a daycare or in school and not take care of any of them, but her own little girl.

I felt bad leaving my son with her and not paying her, since I know how much work taking care of children is, but I had no choice, because I had no money. I found another sales job, that would accommodate my schedule to one in concordance to a school. But by now, I had to find a daycare before starting a job, because my friend's mom was no longer able to care for my son. I had no money for daycare at all. I had applied for the government program that helps to pay daycare, but it was useless. There was a waiting list to get the help and it was years long. I was freaking out!

I prayed earnestly to God to let me put my son in a daycare without paying them money at first. That prayer may have seemed a bit crazy, but to me it felt more possible for that to happen, than for me to get money for a daycare. After much prayer and fasting, I called a daycare that was near the place where I was going to work and asked them if they would let me register my son there, without me paying them any money at first and give me time to work so I can start paying them back. As I heard myself saying my request, I realized how insane that sounded, but amazingly, they said okay! What a miracle that was indeed!

Moreover, I was in the public bus, on my way to the daycare early in the morning, dressed professionally, since I was going to go to my new job after I dropped off my son in the daycare; when suddenly I felt this gooshy white substance land on my suit. My son had just finished throwing up all over me. I was completely frozen in pure panic! How could this happen right now? I had to go to my new job, and I could not be late. I was in the public bus that would take a long time to get to my destination and now I had my son sick and I was a total mess! After a really dragging ride on the bus, we finally got to our stop. It was on front of the daycare. But as I stood on front of the daycare, I knew that I could not drop him off that day. He was very sick. I had to take care of him now. I also could not go to work with vomit all over my clothes, I would have to go back home to change clothes if I wanted to do anything that day. But for me to go home and change was a huge challenge. The bus takes forever to take me to places. It was for sure not going to happen for me that day. I was not going to go to my new job and my son was not going to be in a daycare. I was obligated by fate to stay home and care for a baby one more time, whether I liked it or not, agreed with it or not, it was not my choice!

I was so frustrated and infuriated, I felt I was going to explode that day. Instead of walking toward the daycare, I had to change my route and walk toward a pharmacy that was next to it. I went to the bathroom there and cleaned up a little bit of the vomit on my clothes. Then I went outside and called my sister on the public phone that was outside the place, because I did not have a cell phone. I told her what had just happened to me and I told her with much boldness in my voice that I did not know how God was going to do it, but that today he would give me the money to buy me a car and to move me out from the place I was in, because I desperately needed my own space, even if that space was a small efficiency! My sister replied to me with her voice sounding extremely worried for me and said to me: "Desiree, calm down, I know this is hard, but you know that you are probably not going to get any money

114

today?!" She then continued telling me words that probably were to encourage me, but I was so enraged that I don't remember whatever else she said to me.

After I hung up the public phone and started walking away from it, I ran into an old friend of mine from my teenage years. She was a professional model and we had not seen each other since a very long time. She was very excited to see me, but she rapidly noticed that something was wrong with me. After talking with her a bit, she offered me a ride home. I was so relieved that I wasn't having to wait for a public bus and then be a long time in the bus all over again to get home. As we were driving home, she asked me to please wait for her a minute because she had to make a stop and do something. I said, of course, do whatever you need to do. She stopped at a bank, did her thing, whatever that was, and then we continued driving home. As she dropped me off, I was saying bye to her with all the gratefulness in my heart for giving me a ride. I really thought that was it and that she was leaving. But she stopped me as I was leaving and said: "Here Desiree, this is for you, buy yourself a car." My eyes became wide opened as I was staring at her hands handing me over $2,000 in cash!

I did not know what to do for a moment. How can this be? This woman has not seen me in years and just like that she is giving me this much money? She insisted that I take the money. I did. I was overjoyed. And frankly, I will never forget that day or that good deed. This was incredible! I called my sister and told her: "Guess what? God did it! Just as I told you that He would do today. He gave me the money to move out and to get me a car!" After I explained to her what had happened, my sister was speechless!

The next day I called a friend of mine that worked buying and selling cars in auctions, I had told him to help me buy a car for $800. That was the most I could spend on a car because I needed the rest of the money for an efficiency that cost $500 per month and would require a $500 deposit and of course $200 from the $2,000 was the tithes that belong to God. My friend told me that he can get me a car for that amount of money, but he warned me that a car that price would give me problems. He then said that if I could give him $1,000 instead of $800, he could help me buy a much better car. But as much as I was tempted to take the tithes from God and use it for the car, I resisted the temptation and refused to do that. I insisted to him that all I had was $800 and that I would have to deal with whatever problems that car would bring me later... I was determined to bless God with my obedience, after the amazing miracle that He had just performed. There was no way I would steal His portion of that money, since He was the One who obviously gave me the money. I also knew He was testing me, and I also knew the devil was also testing me. I was determined to obey God even though it hurt so badly. But as I obeyed, and payed my tithes, I felt this immense joy and peace overflow me and my faith in God and in His miracles increased. I had faith that He would help me get through all this. I felt good paying Him the $200. It felt like an honor to me. Besides, is not every day that I get to pay a $200 tithe. I felt that if I obeyed in this one, perhaps more miracles like the one I had just seen would come to me.

And they were, miracles were happening in all sizes. There was a friend of mine from church who used to give me rides and pray with me, a very sweet woman whom had been praying for a long time for a promotion at her job and finally she got it. She then came to me and handed me over her entire first pay check. She told me that God told her to give it to me. I refused to take it at first and felt embarrassed. But she insisted and told me to please not rob her from the blessing of giving it to me. She said she had to be obedient and that she really heard Him say to her to give me her first paycheck of $400. So once again, with a bittersweet type of feeling, I took the check. It always helped a lot! I also gave my tithes to the Lord from that money. I would pay God my tithes from all the money that I earned and all the money that was given unto me as gifts. And if there were times that I absolutely could not pay the tithes, I would write down how much I owed and then I would pay it back eventually and I would not let it be long before paying it back. To me, paying the tithes was my #1 bill to pay.

I got a small car and moved into an efficiency near the church and the daycare. That last sales job that I tried to get became one more job that I could not take or keep, because of what happened with my son getting sick on my first days. I looked for a new job. I could not work in jobs from 9:00 a.m. to 5:00 p.m. that were in offices because I lacked the computer skills or because they mostly required a college degree. I could not work in restaurants or hotels because they gave me weeknights and weekends to work and my son had a different schedule. So I found another sales job. I had to learn to sell art work from door to door. It was very hard to do, since this art frames were heavy to carry. But the schedule was good, and it was the only thing I found that matched my son's schedule for now.

I drove my son to his daycare and began working here. The training was incredible! We learned how to sell art frames in mostly the no soliciting areas. I learned that selling is an art itself and that body language and psychology has much to do with a salesman success. Is almost as if you must become an actor. The best actor you are the more you will sell. Unfortunately, lying is a strong weapon in this job and no matter how good of a salesman you may be, I saw that the ones who sell most are the ones who lie most. Thankfully, I was not forced to lie in this job. If I sold frames, they really didn't care what I would say. Thus, I had good days and bad days. It was from one extreme to the other. So I really could not tell if I was good at this or not. But I kept myself from lying. My boss was a great motivational speaker and trainer and he also decided to pay me salary instead of commission as it was in the beginning.

My car began to give me problems. Just as my friend warned me. My car was breaking down on me again and again. My boss had to send the tow truck to come and get me a couple of times and he also took my car to the mechanic and payed $400 to fix it. My son also got sick again. Daycare was not a great place for him to stay without colds. He would get sick and I would have to miss work and care for him. He had several feveral seizures and after a couple of them, I had to stay with my son in the hospital for two weeks. I missed work and of course did not get paid and I still had to pay the daycare for all the weeks that he missed, because it did not matter if he did not attend the daycare, I still had to pay.

And as if my life could not be any more challenging, my son's father, instead of helping me out, decided to take me to court to try to take custody of my son. As I am in the middle of trying to figure out how I am going to pay my rent, because of how many days I missed of work, now I have this huge mountain to climb.

Before going to work at 8:00 a.m., I would wake up at 4:00 a.m. and go to church. I would pray from 5:00 a.m. to 7:00 a.m. with my son sleeping in my arms as I would walk across the halls of the church back and forth praying. I then would drop off my son in his daycare and go to work, hoping that my car would not break down on me. I would walk all over Miami with this huge art frames and play the role of a sales woman. I had to sneak into places where I was not wanted; and try to sell them a piece before getting kicked out.

But now, I not only had to miss work because of my car breaking down, or my son getting sick, or because of having to go to the Children's and Family Department to try to get food stamps and Medicaid for my son, now I also had to miss work because I had to find a lawyer that the government gave to people like me in Legal Aid and work with them so that I can keep my son with me. All these errands can only be done during weekdays, while my son was in daycare, and at the same time that I was at work. I missed so many days of work is unethical in any boss's mind, but thankfully, my boss was patient and liked me enough to help me. I did not lose my job because of his kindness.

However, my efficiency had to be paid and I was short of $300 because of all the days I spent at the hospital. A friend of mine from church was kind enough to lend me the money. All the money I had went to pay the daycare because without daycare I am at a dead end!

I was so stressed out! I was sleeping very little as usual. My body felt so tired. I remember one morning in the prayer meeting, I was walking back and forth with my son in my arms as he slept, and I had to carry him, or he would wake up from the noise. As I was carrying him, I was telling God that I thought I was going to have to stop coming to the prayer meetings in the morning because my arms were so tired. My son was getting heavier by the day and those art frames at my job were killing me. I prayed this prayer inside my mind. No one there was listening to me, and out of nowhere, this man who also assisted these meetings regularly came up to me and told me: "The Lord says that is necessary that you come to these meetings every morning, He says He will give you strength in your arms to continue to come."

I truly was about to quit that day. That day was going to be my last time going there, during that season of my life, because I was too tired, but because of that prophecy, because of how precise it was and the timing of it was right after my prayer, I decided to continue going there.

CHAPTER 9

LEARNING TO WALK
ABOVE THE WATERS

My life began to feel like a real-life video game. God placed me in the most vulnerable situations that would make any grown man cry. He really made it clear that without Him and His grace, I was not going to be able to make it. Learning to live by faith and on my knees was no longer an option for me. It was a matter of life and death. My art sales job was still good for me in the financial aspect of it, however, there came a problem with my boss. He was a good looking man who just loved women a bit too much. He was a married man and had a son and another child on the way. He seemed to like me a bit too much. Although it worked in my favor because he was being extremely patient with all my car drama and all the sick days my son had which kept me out of work, but in the other hand, when I was working with him, he was too flirtatious with me. He would say things that would stir up my flesh and since he was helping me out so much, it was causing me to feel attracted to him. I fought my flesh against all of that and tried to keep my distance, but it began to get extremely challenging, since we worked together and spent a lot of time together, sometimes we were left alone in the office too. I fasted and prayed to God to help me to work there without falling into temptation, but the Lord was starting to deal with me about it and telling me to leave the job or that I would fall in temptation with him.

I was so tired of having to start looking for a new job, that the thought of quitting this job made me sick to my stomach. The thought of having to be unemployed for God knows how long all over again, made feel like I wanted to throw up. I also knew that quitting this job, even if it was for a good and moral reason, would mean nothing but trouble for me. People will only believe even more that I just don't want to work and that I am lazy and crazy. I really thought about it and decided that instead of quitting I would just fast and pray harder. But one day, we were alone in the office and he hugged me, and my flesh was as weak and vulnerable as can be. I just was lonely, needy and had not been with a man for a long time. In the middle of the hug, I remembered God warning me that if I didn't quit the job, I was going to sin. Suddenly, a rush of fear crept all over me and I stepped back and made my decision. I quit. I let him know that I appreciated all he did for me, but that I was a Christian and that I felt tempted by him and that the best thing to do was to leave the job. I also thought about his wife and children and that I certainly did not want them to go through what I was going through because of my selfishness. Thus, even though I needed the job and I had no idea how I was going to pay my bills once again, once again I chose to obey God and depend on Him and not on money. I knew that it would be painful thou, and I cried a lot after quitting. I also missed my boss. He had become my friend by then and I had gotten used to his company. But like a drug, I had to give him up to the Lord, and so I did!

Shortly after this, the people that were renting me the efficiency I was in, sold their home. I had no choice but to move out. At first, I had no money to move, so the church paid for me to stay at a motel for a week. I started a job at Liberty Tax, but it was seasonal. I was only hired there for a couple of months. When my son's father found out that I was staying at a motel with my son, he became enraged and took me to court. When we went to court that morning the judge had canceled it because of some personal reason. My lawyer then said to me than in her entire twenty years of working as a lawyer, she had never seen a trial canceled at the last minute. She said that if we would have gone through the trial that morning, I would have probably lost my son temporarily. She said she was going to start telling her clients to do the same thing I do. To pray! She said it was working!

I then moved in somewhere else. When we went to court for the custody battle, the judge told my son's father, that instead of him taking my son away from me, what he was going to do was to ordain him to pay me child support by the court. Meaning that he would no longer just give me money randomly, whenever he could give me money and then not give me anything because he could not. I was blown away! The judge noticed that his child support was an important detail in my financial disaster. I could not believe it! Common sense has been something that seems to be missing in most people these days.

From here on, my life was on a cycle mode, from fixing my broken car, to staying home and working on healing my sick child, to moving my things from place to place, to looking for new jobs, to missing work days so that I can go to court for custody battles or to see the lawyer, or missing work to go to the Children's and Family Department to get food stamps and health insurance for my son. Also, I missed a lot of work because I was evicted and had to move out or because the people I was renting from moved out... It was a nightmare!

I worked so hard, but in things that did not pay me. It became a privilege for me to be able to be at work and my biggest challenge was no longer making sales; but getting to work and staying in it through the day. Most of the jobs I was able to get were solely on sales commission, so if I worked hard, but didn't sell much, I was as broke as if I just stayed home that day. I began doing the math on the amount of money I was spending in gas, daycare, food and clothes to go to work and I realized that I was paying to go to work. Mathematically wise, I was better off not going out to work.

As time kept passing by, my situation not only wasn't getting any better, to most people it seemed that it was only getting worse. A lot of people in the church began to seriously believe that I was cursed because of sin and that was the reason I could not prosper. I was beginning to see people looking down on me a lot. It became harder and harder for me to socialize. It was just so obvious to me of the level of shame that people stared at me with. I always felt guilty, even though I wasn't guilty, I was doing the best a human being can possible do! Unless, this society believes that the best that a human being can do is to leave under-age children alone at home while you go out to work, or to leave them with really messed up people. Then, if that is the case, I was guilty of that! And it turned out to be that I found out the hard way, that indeed, this society, including so called "Christians" don't accept any excuses when it comes to working. Not even the excuse of not having any-one to care for your child.

I ended up having to drive my car with no insurance on it and even with an expired tag. I had no money for those things. Between daycare and rent, I was left with very little money. In the other hand, God kept on mani-festing His hand of provision in the most amazing ways. All types of people from the church would just randomly come up to me and donate their money to me. They would never cease to shock me to the core! Many of them would always say that "God told them to give me the money." I had people drive to my place from far away and give me money because God told them to do it. I had others come to my place and give me groceries just as it happened in my Apt., I saw miracles after miracles of God's mercy and provision that had me with my jaw dropped open in total shock. I even had a cop once pull me over because of my altered and expired tag and she saw that I also had no insurance or gas. After I explained to her my situation, she not only let me go, she gave me gas money because I was about to run out of gas and gave me her card so that if I got into any other trouble, she would help me out.

Hence, in one hand, I was being devoured by Satan and this system, but in the other hand, I was witnessing the most amazing miracles and signs of God's mercy and grace almost as the people of the Old Testament. My faith was most certainly being molded greatly through all these experiences and most definitely my faith in God was being enlarged enormously.

My son's father would not stop taking me to court to try to get custody of my son and every time we would go, I would keep winning. I was still assisting the prayer meetings, and believe it or not, throughout all that madness, I always served God. I served Him in the church and outside of it. I evangelized souls everywhere I would be. I worked in the daycare of the church as a volunteer every Sunday while the people would go to the service. I chose that ministry so that I can be with my son as I served the Lord, since I was already without him a lot, because of work. I got involved in multiple ministries, throughout the years. In spite of everything that I was going through. I never quit paying my tithes either. I was determined to be obedient to God in everything I can to see if I can come out of what it began to feel a maze with no end.

After stumbling from place to place and job to job, I unfortunately ran into a major dead end. My son was kicked out of his daycare because I owed: $666 of child care payments which I fell behind. When I saw that debt, I certainly took it as a sign that Satan was behind my disgrace. I was stuck without any way out. I was stuck in one of my cousin's home without a clue as to how I was going to be able to come out and work. Who was going to care for my son while I worked? And how in the world would I be able to afford paying for child care and at the same time save up money to move out? It just seemed as a huge mountain for me to climb. And as if my life wasn't challenging enough, my car broke down for good. It was so messed up it would be cheaper to buy another car than to fix mine.

Oh, how I cried during these days! How much did all of that hurt! Then I also had to overhear people gossiping about how lazy and crazy I am and what a disaster of a person I was! It was so painful. It didn't occur to anyone that just going to work to "fix my problem" wasn't as easy as they all thought. It didn't occur to anyone that my baby could not be left all alone or with mentally ill people while I go out to work. Why was it so hard for everyone around me to see the elephant in the room? Why would they all just accuse me and condemn me and mistreat me as if I was happy with my situation? Because the feminist movement has desensitized everyone to the point that it has become more ethical and acceptable to abandon underage children to go to work, than to protect them and never abandon them no matter the cost.

> **And the great dragon was cast out, that old serpent, called the Devil, and Satan, which deceiveth the whole world: and he was cast out into the earth, and his angels were cast out with him. Revelation 12:9**

During my days in captivity in my cousin's house, I used to walk to a neighbor's house that also assisted my church and they had Bible studies once a week. I went every week and after being there for months without having the slightest clue on how God was going to rescue me, a prophetess from the meetings gave me a powerful word. She said: "I see you and your whole family jumping up and down with much joy! Soon you will all receive a huge blessing and the entire family will rejoice. God wants you to know that this blessing will come to all your family because of your prayers. He has seen your tears and heard your clamor and soon you will see His mighty blessing." I had no idea what she was talking about. I could not even imagine. But I believed her and had faith that soon something was going to change my life.

Two weeks later, my grandmother called me from Puerto Rico. She sold a huge land that she owned in Puerto Rico and now she was going to distribute the money with her children and grandchildren. This land had been for sale for decades. It was almost as if it was cursed. They could not sell it or grow any produce from it. But the curse was now lifted and shortly after, my uncle came to Miami and gave me $30,000. Now I was able to move out of my cousin's house after staying in there as if living in probation for seven months. I paid $3,000 in tithes, bought me a $5,000 car, moved into a two bedroom apt and bought new furniture. I paid six months of rent ahead to give me time to get my life in order, thus I gave them $7,000, rent was $1,100 per month. I had nothing when I got the money, thus, getting all that left me with little. But now I was able to try to fix my life once again. I decided to try to get a Real Estate license in hopes that I can get a better paying job. I paid for my school and studied hard. I passed the class, but the test was not so easy for me. As I was in the road to recovery, once again, life throws me a curve ball! My niece, Hailie called me on the phone asking me if she and her mother can move in with me, because they were homeless and hitchhiking from strangers. I was shocked and of course I said yes. They took a bus from GA to Miami and moved in with me. They slept in one room and once again my son had to share rooms with me.

I invested myself in Hailie's mom. She was not a Christian and I took her to church, and preached to her a lot, I prayed for her a lot and she even got baptized. Unfortunately, that didn't last for too long. She ended up going back to her old ways and they were not good. I didn't know what to do. Time was passing by and she had no job and she was not in a good path either. Then in the middle of all this, we got hurricanes coming in like if it was the end of the world. Huge and destructive hurricanes back to back to back. It disrupted many people's lives and getting money was not easy for anyone these days. I ended up working with a Colombian family that lived near me, fixing roofs and fences that had been taken down by the hurricanes. Even though I worked like a man, I was very excited because I was expecting a lot of money. But unfortunately, they scammed me and decided to pocket most of the money and pay me very little. I couldn't believe it! I was so heartbroken! I thought these people were good people. I thought they cared about me. I worked just as hard as all of them, but they decided to do that and so they did.

Now I was in trouble. I started to fall behind in my rent once again. I had used up all my time in studying for the Real Estate License, dealing with Hailie and her mom, and then working for people that promised me the world and robbed me in the end. In the middle of that, I met my upstairs neighbor. He was a very nice guy who had a crush on me. The guy was as persistent as can be in trying to date me. But the whole time, I said no. I was still hurt about losing my son's father and even though his father kept on giving me pure war concerning child support and custody of my son, I was still praying for us to get back together. Mainly because I didn't want my son to grow up without his father. I had faith that maybe God can bring him back to me. But my neighbor had no shame or pride. It seemed to me that the more I would reject him, the more he would desire me. He was good looking and a little older than me. But I was determined to stay away from him. However, he won over the hearts of my son and Hailie. He came over the apt and played with them and he just was fun for them. They absolutely loved him! But with all that fun, he brought me temptation and I once again, I found myself fighting myself to death.

After seven months of living in the apt and trying to resist temptation, once again, I was evicted! Hailie's mom who had just finally started working and Hailie had to move in with another family member, and poor me, I ended up moving with my neighbor. What can I say other than I fell in love with him and I was in big trouble! He was an atheist! I took him to church, and he tried to get into the Lord, but he just could not believe in God. "But he loved me, so he said." He even wanted to marry me. But he was an atheist. And he loved women too much and alcohol too. I was in trouble. Big trouble! I prayed and prayed so hard for God to help me get out of that situation. I prayed and begged God to provide me a way to move out of my neighbor's place and I promised Him that if He would give me the money to move out, I would break off my relationship with this guy, since I knew God did not want us together. Well, God did it! He provided $1,000 through one of His servants and I moved into an apt. I found in the newspaper. I was renting a room in a two bedroom apt with a guy who also had a little son. I was terrified that I had to move in with a total stranger who was a male, but I was desperate. I moved in and the agreement was to pay $500 per month.

The battle was on concerning my neighbor. He would not let me go. He kept on coming over to see me and try to be with me. Then Hailie came back begging me to let her live with me again, because the place where she and her mom were, was filthy and they would leave her with my male cousin who is mentally ill. I was so heartbroken concerning Hailie's situation, but I was with my hands tied. I was trying to survive myself. I told her I could not take her anymore. It was just too much. I barely had food to eat for my son and myself and Hailie's parents would never give me any money to help me out when I would have her. But she would not take no for an answer. She was so unhappy where she was staying that she begged me to let her stay with me. Her mom was always working or out and she spent too much time alone or with my cousin, a mentally ill grown man. So even though I really had no money, I said okay. I moved her in with me. There were days where I remember buying Hailie and my son food at a fast food restaurant and I would sit on front of them watching them eat, while I starved, because I had no money for me to eat. I survived on the food baskets my church would pass out randomly and I remember not eating very healthy.

I began to believe that I was cursed by now. I began to believe that indeed there was something that I was doing wrong. That perhaps there was sin in my life that I was not aware of. Why was I constantly in poverty? Why was it so hard for me to get money through work? I would fight these intrusive thoughts all the time. After a couple of months of living in this room, the roommate whom I rented from was being evicted and had not said anything to me. It turned out that he owed a lot of months of rent and now we all had to move. He took off without saying anything to me and once again I had to find a new place to live.

I ended up moving into a small apt a friend of mine had with her husband and two kids. This time I took Hailie with me. I could not give her up. I was torn in pieces. This friend of mine was also poor and struggling, she really could not afford to help me, but she did. When I got there, the apt was filthy. I spent the whole first week cleaning that place up because it was unbearable to live in those conditions. Then I had no idea what I was supposed to do. I now had two kids, no money for child care and how was I supposed to work? Who would take care of them, while I work?

It wasn't long for my friend to freak out on me and kick me out. After she kicked me out, I went for a walk, with only my cell phone in hand. As I wept and prayed, I asked God, "So now what I'm I supposed to do? Where are we supposed to go?" And suddenly, a good friend of mine whom I had not spoken to for years, just happened to be thinking of me and she decided to call me up. When she spoke to me on the phone, I told her my situation and she moved me in with her and her husband. She was the friend of mine who had helped me take care of Hailie during her first years of life. I moved in with them and we all had one room and slept in one bed. Hailie, my son and me. I slept in the middle of them and I was very uncomfortable, but they were being cared for and happy. I woke up every morning at 4:00 a.m. and drove my kids with me to the prayer meetings at the church. They would be sleeping the whole time, in their PJs. They had sleeping bags and I would lay them down on the carpet by the seats and pray over them from 5:00 a.m. to 7:00 a.m. Then I would take them to the church's bathroom, and they would change into their school uniforms and from there I would drive them to their school, and they would eat breakfast in their school. Their school was far from the house we lived in now, but since we moved around so much, I didn't want to change their school. Their school was the most stable thing in their life. Especially for Hailie. So for me to save gas money, I would drive to the Public library near their school and work on the computer or read and write while I waited for them. Then I would pick them up and drive them back into the library and sit with them and help them do their homework. After a couple of hours of doing homework, we would drive home again and eat dinner, shower and sleep to do it all over again at 4:00 a.m. the next day. Every so often, my neighbor whom I dated would show up and try to date me again, but I was being hard to get again. Although, he did cause me to stumble from time to time.

Seven months after, my friend and her husband sold their home and moved to GA. Hailie moved back with her mom and I paid the Colombian family I had worked for previously $1,000 that the Lord provided for me, so I can stay there for a little while. This was in the beginning of the summer and I was just utterly tired of my never-ending cycle. I called my son's father and asked him to take my son with him for the summer so that I can fix my life once and for all. I was sure he would say yes and take him, since that was what seemed to me the only thing he cared about. But to my surprise, he said he could not take him because he had to work, and he had no one to take care of my son. He suggested that I send my son to Peru and that his mother would take care of him. But Peru was way too far for me to do that. I could not do that. Thus, I kept my son and we slept in the kid's room in this tiny two bedroom apt that they had. They were four children, plus my son and me in this tiny room. It was summer time and the kids would watch TV all night long. To top it all off, instead of focusing on work, I had to do major community hours because of tickets I had gotten for driving without a proper tag and insurance. It was a never-ending nightmare!

This place was so hard to be in, that even though in the beginning of this summer, I had determined myself to stay away from my neighbor to the point that I threw my cell phone into a lake so that I would have no way of speaking to him, once again my persistent, romantic neighbor came into my life when there was no other way out for me and saved the day. He didn't care that I got rid of my phone, he would drive to where I was and look for me and I ended up moving back with him. And just like that, I had to start from scratch all over again.

In the middle of my chaos, one night, a friend of the family came and knocked on my door and handed me over Hailie. She told me her mother left and that she could no longer look out for Hailie. So I brought Hailie in with me and I was furious at both of her parents for making her and me go through all this pain! All her clothes smelled like cigarettes. I spent all night washing her clothes and folding them. I had to ask my neighbor to be patient with me and luckily for me he allowed Hailie to stay with us in his one-bedroom loft. I was so stressed out! She didn't stay long with us. Her mother came and picked her up again after coming back from Disney World. There was nothing I can do. As usual, I could only hope and pray she would be okay.

I ended up getting a seasonal job asking for voter's signatures and the only reason I did well was because my neighbor took care of my son and even picked him up for me when I could not make it on time at the daycare. Hailie was back with me again, and my neighbor ended up taking care of her for a little while also. I also used to bring her with me to work and taught her how to do what I did, and she did it and was great at it! I would pay her $100 a day. I was able to make enough money to move into an efficiency and once again I began the process of forgetting about my neighbor, which was never easy for me; He ended up getting a new girlfriend. When I found out about this girlfriend, I was devastated, because even though I was planning on leaving him, I loved him. I thought he also loved me. But he was not as in love with me as I thought after all. He told me he knew that I was going to leave him and that he can't be single and that was why he got this new girlfriend, but that didn't stop him from trying to have me back. He used to continue to look for me. To the point that I had to make a decision, either I would put a restriction order on him, or

I would notify his girlfriend whom lived in his apt that her new boyfriend was tempting me to sin with him. I chose to write his girlfriend a huge letter and that was the end of that. I was desperately trying to walk in the spirit and to be in obedience to God so the enemy cannot continue to do what he was doing to me and my neighbor seducing me to sleep with him had to come to a complete halt! Finally, I moved into an efficiency together with Hailie and my son.

CHAPTER 10

MIAMI DADE COLLEGE

Once I settled in my new place, I started assisting college. I knew that financially wise going back to college was not realistic, because I really didn't have the money to do this, but I was determined that by faith, somehow, God will allow me to go back to school and finish what I had started many years ago. I was very upset that my entire future had been violently ripped away from me because of my mother's illness and all the other tragedies that I experienced during my first years of college. I believed that I was meant to graduate from college, and this was going to be the time for me to accomplish this dream. Throughout the summer while I worked, I also invested a lot of my time figuring out how to go back to school. I applied for student loans and a bunch of other things so that I can see if it would work out for me.

I knew that to continue the route I was in was a major dead end and it would surely take me down to the grave. I needed a real career if I ever wanted to get out of my poverty. I needed to figure out a way on how to get me a college degree so that I can put an end to all my hardship. I ended up qualifying for a full scholarship and student loans. The only catch to this was that I had to go to school full time. I knew this was going to be incredibly hard since I had Hailie and my son to take care of and provide. I knew that college is not easy at all. It takes a lot of time and hard work. I already had gone to college. I knew that working even in a part time job would be impossible. Simply because I needed to pick up the kids every day after school and be with them and in weekends I had to take care of them as well. My time was limited and the only free time I ever would have, would have to be used to work on my homework from school.

I still decided to go ahead and do it. I prayed a lot about it and God gave me a dream with me walking around the college with my bookbag. That dream was my confirmation from Him that He would get me through it somehow. Thus, I registered for the first semester and was able to get in school with all my classes paid and my books. I was so happy! My joy was beyond comprehension. I felt like a teenager all over again. I was excited that perhaps now my life would finally change for good. I was also so happy to be around so many young people. I had been surrounded by adults in my churches and jobs for a very long time and this new experience of going back to school was just so refreshing. It was so nice to see all these young faces full of expectations. I also love learning. I love writing and reading and listening to lectures about all kinds of subjects. Thus, I felt as a little girl in a park!

However, as everything in life is, even though I was excited and happy, I did not always feel that way. As time went by, it got scarier and scarier because I sometimes didn't have any gas money, or my car insurance and tag were expired, and I had no money to renew it. I drove with my heart on my throat many days. I had to park far away so that I would not get tickets or towed away and sometimes I had to ask for gas money to total strangers. One time in a gas station, a man offered to marry me for papers and offered me a whole lot of money. Of course, I said no! That was not the first time this happened to me. Temptation to get money in immoral ways was always there for me, but with the grace of God, I always managed to say no. Not only did I say no, I also managed to continue to pay my tithes and offerings faithfully. I paid tithes from my student loans as well. I will be honest with you, paying my tithes in such desperate situations became the hardest thing for me to do sometimes. But I still did it anyway. My days consisted of going to the prayer meetings at 5:00 a.m. at my church, I would take the kids asleep in their pajamas and they would sleep in sleeping bags while I would pray over them. Then at 7:00 a.m. the kids would get ready for school in the church bathroom and then I would drive them to school and they would eat breakfast there. From there I would go to my school and be there all day in my classes, then I would go back to pick up the kids in their school and drive them back to the efficiency. The drive was very long because unfortunately we had moved very far from their school, but I did not want to change them from their school, so I suffered the gas money situation like crazy.

I remember one time driving them home from school, I had worship music playing on the radio. Hailie and my son were sitting on the backseat and all of the sudden, I looked and found Hailie and my son crying, hugging each other and asking for their dads. Oh, just writing this right now brings tears down my eyes. I was blown away by this! I don't know if the music stirred their emotions, but they were both balling and asking why it was that they didn't have their fathers with them? I could not do anything but drive and hear them cry. The ride was very, very long.

After school, we would get home and I had a routine with them. They showered and I would cook for them and they would eat and then do homework. I would clean up and put all of us to sleep by 9:00 p.m. I woke up every morning at 4:00 a.m. to be at church at 5:00 a.m. And then we would do it all over again. I remember that when I started college, I had to make a decision about church once again. The people in the church all participated in many activities almost every week night and in the weekends. But the problem was that all those activities were interrupting my schedule with my kids. I could not do both, I could not be a good mother and a homemaker, a full-time college student and involved in all the church programs that we were all supposed to be involved in. I decided to quit everything in church except the prayer meetings in the morning, the Sunday morning services and the Monday night school for ministers. I assisted the Institute of Leadership of King Jesus Ministries for over six years. I had to do it really slow because of my kids and I only was able to get the first diploma. I took a lot of classes and passed them for the highest diploma, and I was only four classes away from graduating with the highest diploma, but I had to quit all together in the end.

I still felt pretty rejected by the church for choosing to opt out from serving in the night services and from joining the house of peace and discipleship programs that they had. But I knew that God Himself preferred that I focused on getting my classes passed and taking good care of the kids and not stopping from praying earnestly. I was so overloaded with things to do already, considering that I was mother and father to Hailie and my son and that I had no government help whatsoever coming to me for Hailie, since she was not legally mine. I also had no child support from any of her parents and my son's father would sometimes take long to pay his child support and his child support has always been under $400 a month. The level of stress that I was under was intense and luckily for me I was still young and full of energy and boldness. It took all my energy and boldness just to pick up my keys and drive with an expired tag and no insurance and sometimes with my license suspended because of it. But I had to drive. I had no choice. I had to take the kids to school, and I had to try to get me a degree. There was no other option for me. Just as the option of leaving my niece and my son all alone when they were still in Elementary school so that I can go to work was never, ever an option for me either.

I was determined to do things with integrity on front of God and I didn't care what anyone else thought of me. All I knew is that my only options to do this thing was by driving illegally and without much gas money. On front of God, that was more holy than to choose to leave the kids alone or with crazy people to go to work. And why were these my only options? Because the society we live in has a rigged system. This rigged system sets us up to fail as parents, as children of God and as moral people. The moment the feminist movement was implemented, they set all of us up to fail! In God's Biblical society, I would have never gone through anything like this. Because in His holy society, women were never expected to work. They were homemakers and they were taken care of by their fathers and husbands. Also, orphans were well taken care of as well and Hailie sort of became an orphan because of the gross neglect coming from both her parents. But here I was in the modern world, with no father, no husband, no mother, and a niece that was in my same exact situation, but without being an adult.

Unfortunately, since now a day's women are expected to work and maintain themselves, people have forgotten about the single mothers like myself and about the orphans like my niece. Although, my niece technically had her parents alive, they were nowhere to be found most of her life and she grew up with me most of her childhood.

Moreover, I could not participate in the church activities. And sitting down on their temple and listening to their sermons became more and more painful to me each time, because they got so consumed with all the serving in the church and all their programs and activities, that their sermons converted more and more into a recruiting session for volunteers and a condemning session for those folks as myself that were opting out from serving in their church. However, I still chose to continue going and enduring all the criticism and condemnation that came to me constantly, for the sake of God. But I was in major pain, especially when I would hear from the pulpit that if "you don't work, you don't eat" as if that was meant for women, when it wasn't, since when Paul said that it was in a time where women were homemakers. It was very painful to also hear that if you don't serve in the church you are useless!

Furthermore, I was doing good in my classes and the kids were also doing well in theirs. Then one night, my son got sick and once again he suffered a seizure from his fever. It was really late in the night and I now had to spend the rest of the night in the hospital with my son and my niece was dropped off at her mother's place by my new neighbor who kindly offered to take her so that she could go to school the next day and not be alone or in the hospital with me. My son was sick for some time and Hailie ended up moving back with her mom. I spent weeks without sleeping, because my son's fever was so aggressive. I did not stop monitoring it and praying over him so that God would heal him. I missed a lot of classes, but thankfully I was able to make up all the work and passed all my classes. An absolute miracle!

I saw the hand of God move mightily in Miami Dade College, He moved on my behalf to help me pass my classes and He also revealed Himself to many people there that I had the honor to meet and lead to the Lord. But the attacks from the enemy did not stop coming against me to stop me from graduating. I even got into a car accident one morning after dropping off my kid in school and as I was on my way to take my final exams. I was hit hard by the back and if I would not have had my seat belt on, I would have gotten really hurt! But I didn't get too hurt, just really startled! I just left the scene and took my test. If I had stayed there, I would have missed my final exam and maybe even fail the class. I had my tag and insurance expired and my license was suspended. I was not going to stay in that car accident to see what would happen. Although, it was a hard crash, my car was an SUV strong car and nothing really happened to me. The car that hit me though, was another story. His front part was by the middle and his car looked really bad. But he hit me by the back while I was totally stopped. It was not my fault and Satan was not going to steal my classes that day from me, oh no! I had studied really hard for that test and I also worked really hard for that entire semester, I needed to get there and get a good grade and so I did!

In another semester, in the middle of another season of final exams, my grandmother who lived in Puerto Rico passed away. The entire family left to Puerto Rico to be at her funeral. I could not go. I had to pass my final exams. I remembered how my mother was the cause of me quitting college last time I went. I was not going to let anyone, or anything make me quit again. To this day I marvel at how many challenges and oppositions came my way to stop me from succeeding in college and how much God helped by doing miracles or simply giving me the guts to do the things I did to simply get to school.

Once again, I was in the middle of studying and pre-paring for final exams when I get the news from Hailie's brand new step father telling me how Hailie's mom just moved back to GA and left Hailie with him. He was heart-broken since they had just gotten married and he knew that she went back to be with an ex-boyfriend, and he was telling me that he did not know what to do about Hailie. I was infuriated by this news and I had just enough of this! I of course, brought Hailie back to live with me and decided to take her mother and her father, who is my brother, to court! I could no longer do this in this manner. If I was going to take care of Hailie, it would be in an orderly manner. Hailie's parents were ruining both of our lives with all this instability toward Hailie. It wasn't fair either that they both collect tax return funds for being Hailie's parents, while I was suffering dire poverty because of having Hailie without the proper financial support.

As much as I love my brother, he gave me no choice, but to take him to court. I applied to take full custody of Hailie and explained the situation about her mother abandoning her with the step-father and they gave me temporary custody. I thought hard about my decision and there was just no other option but to do this. Because she always ended up having no one else to take care of her, but me. Then I would also have to endure all the emotional damage that was being done unto her and try to heal her, and that was a lot of hard and painful work for me. But it was not so much the work that bothered me, since I love her as my own daughter, it was that after I would invest so much time, money and energy on her, her mother would take her back and damage her all over again with her lifestyle. Unfortunately, her mother was a drug addict and suffered mental illness as well.

I had taken care of Hailie so much and for so long that I truly saw her as my daughter. I purposely trained myself to see her as my daughter so that I can do what I did for her. I had to train myself to think of her as my own daughter, so that I don't hurt her by loving my son any more than how I loved her. I wanted her to not feel left out or rejected or indifferent. When she was with me, she was my daughter and I treated her no different than how I treated my son. Always! Also, for me to be able to exercise the patience that I needed with her, it could only be done if I loved her that much. Thus, I trained my mind and heart to see her as my daughter, no buts, or ifs… But this came at a high price, because now I was worried for her as if she was my daughter, but she wasn't. Now, I was terrified every time that her mother would take her as if she was my daughter, but she wasn't. But as the Bible says in **Corinthians: Love suffers everything**!

Thus, after much thinking and much praying, I concluded, that my only option to put an end to all this misery and suffering with Hailie was to take full custody of her. She was eleven years old by now. This disorder needed to come to an end. Whether I got full custody of her or not, I was not going to continue to be Hailie's parent's nanny at no cost. I was not going to continue to allow her parents to neglect her the way they did and just get her back whenever they felt like it. I was no longer going to just passively watch as Hailie lives in filth, with no one attending her, with her mentally ill family member who is too mentally ill to work in formal jobs, yet they see nothing wrong with making him her babysitter. I loved Hailie and myself too much to continue to allow this irresponsible behavior to continue. I never asked to be a parent when my niece was born. I never asked to stay home and care for her while she was just a baby. I was practically forced by their neglect to do this. It had affected me financially my whole life. Yet her parents were too busy in their own world to realize how much suffering I was enduring for the well-being of their daughter. But the time came that I was going to let them know just how hard it has been for me and for Hailie. The time came for me to take a stand and put an end to all of this! And as if my life wasn't painful and hard enough, I had to make sure to get all this done without failing my final exams and continuing to go to my next classes and pass them.

CHAPTER 11

THE COURT CASE

Taking my brother to court was probably one of the hardest things I have ever done. I really love him. No matter what has happened, I used to see him as my own baby when he was really little. Growing up with him, I used to always look out for him and worry about him. My brother used to be my best friend when we were young. We shared many good times together and many friends. Unfortunately, we grew apart and the situation with Hailie drove us further and further from each other. But I never stopped loving him. I never held grudges against him either. I just didn't approve of the decisions he was making concerning Hailie and I could not watch Hailie being neglected and abandoned and not get involved.

Even though I heard time again and again from the people in our lives that I needed to stop taking care of Hailie and worrying about her, that she wasn't my daughter and to mind my own business, I could never do that. I held her in my arms while she was an infant, she also happened to be the angel God placed in my life to bring me out of my depression when my mother passed away. She was my first child. She called me mommy for many years. I saw her take her first steps, I was there to comfort her when she had her ear infections, when no one else did. I was the one that drove her to church and took care of her day in and day out, I spent sleepless nights with her in my arms when she was sick. How can I just turn a blind eye to her neglect? How can I just go on with my life and ignore her, knowing she is exposed to danger? How can I mind my own business when she is the one who called me repeatedly to take her in with me, because she had nowhere else to go and when she was homeless with her mom? When she was left with the step father or mentally ill family member? What kind of human being would I be if I just neglect her too? No! Hailie was either going to bring the worst out of me or the best out me. I was not going to let the Devil hardened my heart by me choosing to be selfish and not fight for her and not try to take care of her to the best of my ability. If I was thrown by destiny into her life, it was for a reason and I was going to make sure that I would honor God with the way I treated the most beautiful little girl I have ever met.

Hence, I wrote the judge a huge letter describing my situation with Hailie and he replied by giving me temporary custody of her. I chose to take the opportunity to get Hailie's parents attention. I knew that the court would make copies of the letter I wrote to the judge and give it to both of them. I knew they would read it all since they knew that the judge read it. This letter was very long and descriptive and even though I knew it was a bit too long, I did not care, because I had planned for Hailie's parents to go on a journey where they must see things from my point of view. I also decided to ask all my friends, Hailie's teachers, school bus driver and anyone who knew us to write a short letter to the judge as well. They did. They all wrote the same things. The only parent they knew that Hailie had was me. They wrote about how they always saw Hailie with me and that she lived with me most of her life and that I was the one who maintained her and drove her to school and was with her. I had a huge stack of letters and I gave a copy of all of them to Hailie's parents. I also had Hailie's sister's grandmother from another father write letters saying how she was also trying to take custody of Hailie's younger sister because her mother was unstable and exposed them to dangerous situations and she sent me a court indictment Hailie's mother had concerning another little girl that she has with another father. That child was legally removed away from her by court permanently. The paper said that she lost full custody of that child because she was a danger to herself and her child. I explained to the judge how I was going to college to try to get a good job and that I presently wasn't working because I was going to school full time and then taking care of the kids after school. I brought him all my papers from my classes from both Miami Dade and the Institute of Leadership of King Jesus Ministries. I showed him that I lived in my own efficiency and provided for him so much paper work and letters to prove that I was not only a serious mother trying to provide for Hailie and my son, but also there were so many letters from everyone else confirming that about me and confirming to the judge that both Hailie's parents were neglecting her and not fit to have her.

My brother was paying $600 child support by court all these years, the only problem with that was that Hailie would never see that money because she was with me most of the time. And I never, ever got any child support from any of them. Whenever Hailie was with her mother, that money was not going to her either because her mother would spend it on drugs and alcohol. Her mother would lie to Hailie and tell her my brother was not sending them money. I invested a lot of my time and energy and money on this trial. I prayed a lot about it too. I was terrified! It was very scary to me to venture on with this plan. But I thought that for the sake of Hailie and out of love for her, I really had to choose to be brave and do this. I knew I would hurt my brother deeply by doing this to him and it really hurt me to have to do this to him, but he gave me no choice. He decided that Hailie was better off living with her mother and no matter how many times that decision proved to be incorrect, he continued to leave her with her mom, whom spend little time with her and neglected her, causing me to have to take her with me. I took them to court to also clean my own conscience. If anything, bad, (God forbid), ever was to happen to Hailie, I needed to make sure that I did everything that was in the power of my hands to prevent it. I needed to know that I fought to protect her one hundred percent. So I can sleep at peace at night.

I had so much evidence to proof my case, so many witnesses and certified letters to confirm the things I was claiming that I was almost certain I would win the case and adopt Hailie. The thought of officially adopting Hailie for good also terrified me to death as well. Hailie had many emotional problems due to the way she had been living and she was a lot of hard work for me. She was not like a normal child. She suffered from panic attacks, fears, rejection, malnutrition, depression and was very emotionally unstable. I knew that what I was signing myself up for was going to be a lot of pain and hard work. I also thought about my son. I was going to risk my son being influenced by her bad behavior and rebellious ways. I was going to expose him to her tantrums and emotional roller coaster rides, which may later affect him as well. I also thought about the fact that having Hailie permanently will make my chances of finding myself a good spouse that much harder. The more children I would have, the harder dating becomes. Although, I feared that happening, I still chose to do it. I decided to let God take control of this situation and I asked Him that if He wished for me to have her legally, that I would do it, and I would trust for Him to give me the strength to do it well. I thought that if He thought that I should not adopt her, then He would make sure that no matter what I present the court, I would not win. It really was placed in His hands through prayer. But I was going to give the Lord the opportunity to make that choice. I was going to try my hardest to rescue Hailie from a life of neglect, poverty, emotional and mental abuse and instability that she had been enduring. I also did all that to show Hailie how much I really loved her. I wanted her to see that I loved her enough as to adopt her.

To my surprise, a lot of my family members who knew the type of dangers and neglect Hailie had constantly being exposed to, were upset at me for taking her parents to court and for attempting to adopt her. They accused me of doing that solely for money. They claimed that the only reason I wanted to adopt her was so that I would get child support from them. Is incredible to me to see that years of me sacrificing my life for Hailie, by taking care of her at my expense was not enough to show them, that the reason I wanted to adopt her was out of love for Hailie and not for money. But what was more incredible is the level of indifference they all showed Hailie by choosing to turn a blind eye to all the neglect and pain they all saw that little girl endured at the hands of her parents.

All of the sudden, I sadly witnessed many of our family members side with my brother and Hailie's mom and get really upset at me for taking them to court. Even though, I sent them all copies of the paper work and letters that absolutely confirmed that I was right, and that Hailie was in danger. It didn't matter how much evidence I showed them, they refused to take my side and were offended by my decision.

Then, I still held on to some faith toward the Justice System of the United States of America. I thought, that perhaps those family members who became outraged at my decision to go to court for Hailie, would calm down if they would see that the court agreed with me. But to my dismay, after having to stand next to my brother, his new wife, and Hailie's mom in a court of law and testify concerning Hailie, it turned out that I was the fool because I did not have a formal job and that Hailie's mom was the right person for Hailie to live with because she had a formal job. I was horridly blown away!

I did hear the judge tell my brother apart from everyone, in a low voice, that indeed there were many red flags concerning Hailie's mom and that he should be the one to have Hailie, but unfortunately, my brother wanted Hailie to live with her mom and the judge granted him his desire. How do you figure?

After I realized the dark truth that I lost the case, that I looked like an absolute fool, and that now everyone in my family that was angry with me because of this was more convinced than ever that I was still crazy, I was deeply saddened and confused.

Why did God allow this? Why did He not give her to me? How is she better off with a mentally ill and an addict who already lost legal custody of one of her daughters by a court of law and the other sibling Hailie had was also in a court with her grandmother trying to remove her from her care? How does the Justice System of our nation allow such injustice toward Hailie? How can the system fail her so miserably? How does my brother allow Hailie to continue to live the nightmare she was living? How is my family celebrating my loss and Hailie's mom's victory? Has everyone just gone insane?

Perhaps God allowed this to happen to spare me from things He may not want me to endure. But I am certain that it was never His will for Hailie to stay with her mom in the condition they were living. But God is not a dictator. He never forces people to obey Him. In this case, there were many people choosing to do their own will and not God's will concerning Hailie and He allowed them to do as they pleased, but the consequences are there to be reaped in the future. This situation with Hailie just proofs that we live in a corrupt nation with a corrupt system that is designed to produce dysfunctional adults by having them being raised savagely! They remove children away from good homes and they keep children in the bad homes by design. There is an agenda against the United States of America and that agenda is to destroy society from within. Is an agenda that is very subtle, but it targets the family unit.

And the masses have been so deeply indoctrinated with their communist education, that they are pushing this agenda forward like a train wreck! I was deeply wounded through this entire process. Hailie ended up moving to Georgia with her mother and they prohibited her from having any contact with me in person or by phone. I didn't speak with her for years and I had no idea how she was doing all that time as well. It was very painful to me. I lost her and many in my family were very happy with that outcome!

I also lost my brother after that trial! I lost big time. Yet I chose to thank God for allowing me the honor to do what I did, and I have no regrets whatsoever about my decision, even though I lost. Because on Judgment Day, when we all have to stand on front of Almighty God and give an account for Hailie's upbringing, my hands and conscience will be clean and I will be able to raise up my head and look God straight into His eyes and remind Him that I tried my very best to love her and protect her. And I believe He will look upon me, not in shame, but proud of my work with her and that is all that matters to me!

Even though I don't understand why I did not get her, I will continue to praise my Lord, serve Him and walk with Him. I was never upset at God. I was upset with my brother and family and I was upset with the Justice System of our Nation. But I shook off my pain and sadness, I forgave everyone, and I continued with my life.

(FUNDAMENTAL ATTRIBUTION ERROR: The tendency to explain others behavior as a result of personal rather than situational factors. Defensive attribution is a tendency to blame victims for their misfortune, so that one feels less likely to be victimized in a similar way. Blaming victims for their calamities also helps people maintain their belief that they live in a "just world" where people get what they deserve and deserve what they get (Lerner, 1980,1998). Acknowledging that the world is not just and that unfortunate events can happen as a result of chance factors—would mean having to admit the frightening possibility that the catastrophes that happen to others could also happen to oneself. Defensive attributions are a self-protective, but **irrational** strategy that allows people to avoid such unnerving thoughts and helps them feel in control of their lives (Hafer, 2000, Lipkus, Dalbert, and Siegler, 1996). Unfortunately, when victims are blamed for their setbacks, people unfairly attribute undesirable traits to them, such as incompetence, foolishness, and laziness. Work Cited Psychology Applied to Modern Life by Wayne Weiten and Margaret A. Lloyd. Adjustment in the Twenty-First Century Eight Edition. Pg. 178).

CHAPTER 12

MY GRANDMOTHER'S INHERITANCE

Well after I had submerged myself deeply into all that "Hailie drama," I now found myself having to catch up in my classes from college and in my rent. I was behind in my rent for a couple of months and there was just nothing that I can do about it. I ran out of student loan money and I had no way of working because I had no one to leave my son with while I worked. I was so incredibly overwhelmed with stress that I sometimes felt that I was going to have a stroke. Still, by the grace of God, I managed to concentrate in my studies and passed all my classes and the people that I was renting from were Christians whom also assisted my church. They were very loving, and kind and they patiently waited for me to pay them the rent. For a while I had no idea how I was going to pay my rent but trusted that God had a plan on how to do that, since I knew He was the One who placed me in college once again. It was a miracle that I was even able to register back in school, because I had a huge debt with Miami Dade College from when I had attended in 1996. They had told me that I could never register back until I paid that debt. But still, since God gave me a dream where I saw myself walking in the school with a bookbag on my back, I had faith that He would get me in again somehow.

Thus, I persisted in trying to register and a couple of times when I had tried to register back, they would all tell me the same thing. You must pay the debt you owe to be able to register. But I didn't care, I would keep on trying to register until one day, I went and just like that, the computer didn't block me from registering by stating that I had a pending debt. Just like that, it allowed me to go ahead and register for my classes. And once I was registered as a full-time student, I now qualified for the loans and scholarship, and just like that, I was back in school. A total miracle! Well, in the same way, God used the people that I was renting, to help me get through school. They allowed me to live in their efficiency for months without paying my rent. This is how I was able to finish my college years. It was an absolute miracle that they didn't evict me. Then the other miracle came through my beloved grandmother. She passed away and after her passing away, my family received the rest of the money of the inheritance that she left us all. After I received $30k when she was alive, now in this time, I received $40k.

I paid the people I owed rent the money I owed them which was $4,000. I owed them four months of rent which was $1,000 per month. Then I donated to them $2,000 for having been so kind as to wait for me and for not evicting me. I was deeply grateful! They and God saved my college and had it not being for their patience and kindness I would have failed my classes, or I would have had to quit in the middle of going!

I also paid money I owed to other people. $4,000 were paid in tithes. I then began hanging out with my cousin. I will call him Andrew, but that is not his real name. I started to help him get close to God. I moved into a new apt. with two bedrooms. I decided to move Andrew in with me to disciple him in the Lord. He was homeless at the time, and he had been struggling with life for long enough. I was determined to try to help him get his life in order with God. I thought that perhaps God can "fix" him the same way He fixed me. I witnessed firsthand all the mistreatment, neglect, abuse and rejection my cousin grew up in and I truly felt a lot of compassion for him and wanted to help him to heal. A lot of people warned me to not do it, because they knew how evil he was and they said he would repay me back with evil, but I still had faith that maybe God can change his heart. If only I can get him to focus on searching for the Lord, then his heart would change. I invested so much of my time and energy in him. I patiently taught him everything God had taught me, I sat down and taught him the word of God and would answer all his questions, which were a lot. I even asked him to not work in a secular job and just focus for a couple of months on God. I knew he was very undisciplined and that if I demanded for him to work and pay the bills, he would then not have the energy or desire to study the Bible, fast and pray. He had also gotten money from my grandmother and I had asked him to pay his half with that money for a couple of months in advanced, so that we can have him not work. However, he wasted his money right after he got it, and I found out after he was already moved in with me. I then, still decided to have him stay out of work because I just knew that he would not look for God the way he needed to if he had to go to a job. I told him that his job was going to be to look for God. I even made him a schedule to follow and it was all about praying, reading the Bible, going to church and I made it clear to him that resting properly was part of that schedule; because I didn't want him to be too tired when he had to be on his knees praying or reading the word of God, I knew that he would not focus right in doing those things if he was too tired.

At first, it was working wonderfully, he was actually blooming in the Lord. He had an amazing prophetic mantle upon his life, and it was developing. He was very happy and enthusiastic about everything he was experiencing with God. He was changing. He was repenting. He was getting hungry for the truth like I never saw him before. I was impressed! I was so happy. However, unfortunately, he started to join the churches little groups. He got under a mentor, and they started to put him to serve in all these different things. Just as I predicted, the moment he got too busy serving, he stopped praying and reading the Bible. Thus, he began to go back to his old ways.

He stopped following my schedule that I had given him to follow and things with him became a little bit strange. One day, he was praying in the living room and I was in my room, he came into my room and was very startled. Then he suddenly said the words: "Desiree you were raped!" The Lord showed me in prayer that you were raped when you were young but that you have no memory of it because you were drugged by the rapist!" I was horrified by those words.

My heart sunk and I felt like vomiting. I remembered a prophecy someone once told me that something really terrible happened to me when I was a teenager but that I don't have the memory of it. I also remembered that the guy who first brought me to Christ while I was schizophrenic, he used to always write poetry and some of his poetry said that I was drugged and raped, but I never thought he meant it literally. He was a very dramatic dark poet and he used to use a lot of strong words to describe things, so I thought when he wrote that, he was just describing my spiritual condition in a very dark style.

I started to cry and freak out. I cried nonstop for three days. I even had suicidal thoughts. I fell into a deep depression. Then one day, someone introduced me to a woman of God. I met this lady and the first time we ever met, she began prophesying things to me about my life. She said that she saw that I had a curse upon my life. That she saw that I would get financial blessings but then I would go back down to being poor. She said that she saw that no matter what I did, something always would pull me back down. She said this was because of my ancestors. She said that my ancestors were very wicked and that they had done blood covenants with Satan for money and power and that it was sacrifices to a high level to get positions in the government. I couldn't believe it! How did this woman know so much about me? She described my situation to the teeth. I was blown away about how detailed she was. She then mentioned to me of a liberation group that worked in Peru. She advised me to go to them so that they can deliver me. I told her I had already been delivered by the Pastors of my churches. But she said that these people were different. She said I wasn't completely delivered yet. She said these people go to the third heaven in the spirit and they are revealed all the sins of our ancestors that give legality to Satan and his demons to torment us and defeat us. I was so desperate, that I agreed to go. I wanted to go more than anything to find out if I had been raped or if that was all a lie. I needed to find out the truth about that more than anything else and I wanted to know who in the world raped me?

I traveled to Peru. I stayed with the lady who prophesied to me and her family. I was ministered by the group in Peru. They gave me a list of all of my ancestor's sins that were giving legality to Satan with my life and I could not be anymore horrified. I come from a very satanic family tree. One of my great grandfathers was a Satanic Priest and performed human sacrifices of children. No wonder most of my family is so lost and messed up! These people were different than every other liberation team I had ever known. They had a huge drawing that the Lord showed them of the places of captivity where the Devil still had my soul in the spirit. The way they did the liberation was by sitting me in a chair and they all sat around me and they all began to pray silently, while the Pastor would communicate the things the Holy Spirit was showing him concerning the place of captivity where my soul was and his assistant would also speak on behalf of the Holy Spirit giving instructions on how to rescue me out of this spiritual regions of captivity. The whole time I was awake, conscious and just peacefully looking at everyone else do their thing with great curiosity. There must have been like thirty people in the room with me. Men and women. No one laid any hands on me and no one was speaking too loudly. I wasn't going crazy and moving uncontrollably as I did during my first liberations. I felt nothing. I was just a spectator in this whole ordeal. Then another day, I was taken into a room with only the Pastor and two women who were his assistants. Here the Pastor commanded the spirit of one of his assistants to place herself in the gap for me and she became as if possessed by me. I couldn't believe my eyes. It was as if I was watching a movie and as if I was observing an actress playing me. They then started asking her questions about when I was in the womb of my mother, what happened that hurt me. This woman began speaking as if she was a little child, saying that she heard my father telling my mother that he wanted her to abort me. Then she began looking as if she was going to start crying. Then the Pastor asked her: "What happened to you during your first years of life up to seven years old?" Then, she replied saying that someone my parents had left me with, sexually molested me. Then she also said that a demon would appear to me every so often and scratch me with his long nails and make me bleed and then he would lick my blood and as he was licking my blood, he would say that I was his food. As I was observing all this going on, I was experiencing all kinds of emotions. I was blown away that I was looking at myself in someone else, and then I was blown away about all the things that happened to me that I didn't even know. Then the Pastor asked her again what happened to me during my teenage years that hurt me? Keep in mind that I never mentioned to any of these people about my getting raped situation. Thus, to my horrific surprise, the woman starts talking once again as if she is possessed by me and starts to say: "What's happening to me? I can't feel anything and then she said, "Oh, no don't hit me! I have no strength!" and she acts as if she fainted. Then the Pastor goes on asking her more about my latter years, and she mentions a quote that I used to always say a lot to myself: "No matter how hard I try is useless!" Oh Lord, I was so scared and sad by now by everything that I had been hearing, I wanted it to stop, but I knew that I must continue. This statement that she said, came from when I was a young adult trying to provide but no matter how hard I worked it never seem to be good enough. By the end of the session, the Pastor and the two women were crying together with me. The Pastor said he had never seen such a sad life in all his life. They revealed to me that the part where the assistant fainted was because they had drugged me, hit me and then I fainted and then five guys raped me!

Even though I went there to find out the truth about that, the truth didn't make me feel better at all. I felt worst that it had been confirmed. I fell deeper into depression. I was angry at the world. I felt tired of life and pure dissolution. However, I had to think about my son. Also, I know the truth about hell and suicide. I was not going to hell for eternity after all I have suffered here on earth. I must be strong and shake all of this off and move on. I came back home and found myself dealing with my cousin Andrew once again. It turns out that since in the church they always preach that women are to submit to their husbands, and that since men are the head of the home and never the women, now he claimed that because of him being a male, he was the head of our home and that I needed to submit to him. Not considering the fact, that I was the one financially maintaining both of us and that he didn't even have a job.

This is the problem with today's feminist society and with the church trying to fit in our feminist society in the biblical society. In the biblical society, women did not have jobs and men were the sole providers, this was the reason why they were the head of the women. The Golden Rule is: "He who owns the gold makes the rules!" The Money Masters Documentary. But the moment the women are the providers and the men are not, then the women automatically becomes the head, not the men. Or do you not see anything wrong with a man being financially maintained by a woman and telling her to submit to him? And if both the man and the woman work and pay the bills, then the fair thing is for both to be the heads. Which is why is so problematic to be married in this feminist world, because no one wants to follow, and everyone wants to lead. But when the man works and pays the bills, then the woman should follow his lead, like in a Tango Dance! It flows beautifully when both of them love each other and serve each other in humility and appreciate each other's role, without under minding the value each brings into the relationship, even if both of them perform different tasks and roles.

I then asked him to start working and paying the bills with me, because my money ran out and I had to pay the entire rent by myself. He didn't get a job, and we ended up getting evicted from that apt.

Moreover, my son's father had told me that he needed a roommate and was in dire need of financial help to keep his two-bedroom apartment. He offered me to move in with him and to help him pay it. I explained to him that my only income was my student loans, financial aid and the child support that he paid me. I told him that until

I finish my college, I was not going to be able to work, because I was attending school full time and then I had to be with our son, since I had no one to leave him with.

He wanted for me to rent his room for $500 a month and he said that he was so tight in money that he may not be able to pay me the child support. Since he was ordained by the courts to pay me monthly and since he knows that when he stops paying me, they persecute him… "Eventually"! (Because the courts have allowed him to owe me all the way up to $2,000 several times).

I decided to tell him: "Well, so that you don't stop paying me your child support money and so that you don't get in trouble with the courts, let me move in with you as your roommate and let me pay you from the child support you give me every month, as I have done in other apts." "It would be as if we were two strangers living together, and you continue to pay me my child support and then I use that same money to pay you my rent. This way I can continue to go to school and you can continue to stay in your place."

He happily agreed and I rephrased the words: "Remember, that the only way we can do this, is if you continue to pay me your child support and you allow me to use that money to pay you the rent." Again, he happily agreed and out of desperation for my own situation, I decided to trust him and move in with him.

Shortly after moving in with him, he began to fight me about money and to make a long story short, we fought like cats and dogs, because as usual, in this feminist world, apparently, no one can understand that underage children can't be left home alone while parents work or that placing your child under a trusted individual or facility, while you go to work, isn't as easy as everyone would like to think. I was living under so much stress during these days and somehow under all that pressure, I still managed to miraculously pass all my classes again. In the meantime, my son's father went as far as to go to the courts and claim that he wanted his child support payments to be removed, because we were living together, and my son was with him and I didn't want to work! Unbelievable! The level of greed in everyone in my life never ceases to amaze me. After I repeatedly told him that I would not move in with him, unless he allowed me to pay him with my child support money coming from him and I repeatedly specified that I needed to finish school before getting back to work, he still went ahead and did that!

Seven months later, we were having to move out. All of us! I had arranged to move into an efficiency and planned on paying my rent the same way I always paid it, with the child support money and the school money. I was getting new student loans each semester. I found a single mom in a home near my area and she offered me an efficiency for the same price, $500. She accepted me and there it is, I was ready to move out and into a new place. My other cousins came to help me get my things and we went to this lady's house. But in my life, nothing is what it seems. There is somehow a curve ball heading my way every so often, just to keep me on my toes and it just never seems to stop coming my way. Just when I thought I was going to finally get some relief and just work on improving my life, this lady decided that she no longer wanted me to move in with her. Just like that, she had me on front of her door, with all my things waiting to be moved into her place and with all my cousins there waiting for me to go, and just like that, she told me, sorry, I changed my mind.

I was so embarrassed. I was tired. I was so confused. I was also very homeless. My cousin Scarlett, (not her real name), who is Andrew's sister, offered me to stay with her for a couple of days while I can find a new place. When I saw that I had to go stay over her home, I just wept with so much agony. I knew that was never a good thing. But somehow, I also knew that this had all been planned by God Himself, and the thought of that made me cry in much more anguish. I even had a vision of myself being crucified just as Christ was crucified, as I wept and cried because I had to stay with my cousin Scarlett.

CHAPTER 13

SCARLETT'S HOUSE

Although, I was extremely grateful and thankful that my cousin was kind enough to let me stay in with her, I was also utterly terrified to be in her home. She lived with my other cousin, her older brother, the mentally ill family member who was Hailie's designated babysitter, who her parents had no problem leaving her with, just as his rest of his siblings would hand over their children for him to care for while they all did their own thing.

I will also change his name. We will call him Johnny. My cousin Scarlet lived with my other cousin Johnny who is mentally disabled, and she also lived with her mother. The house was a really big, beautiful home with three bedrooms, an office and a pool. However, she loved animals and the house was full of dogs, cats, reptiles, birds, even a rabbit at one point lived in there with us. This was extremely difficult for me, because there was a lot of urine smell all over the house and it was unbearable. The dogs that she had were not being walked daily as they should have been, and the house was a pure mess. Also, my cousin

Johnny was there with his own little dog who was a menace and would pee all day long, inside the home. Moreover, Johnny was really messy too and her other brother, my other cousin who was the youngest of them all, "Andrew" would also come over and even lived in there from time to time and he also was very messy, and the house was truly in dire need of a full time maid.

As soon as I moved in, before I can try to start to look for a new place for me to move into, I had to start cleaning up the house, because like I said the smell was unbearable. I also started walking all the three Shitzu dogs that she owned, daily. I also bathe them all and kept them groomed. It would take me all day long just to keep her living room and kitchen area clean. Then I began to look for an efficiency to move into, but no one wanted to take me because I didn't have a formal job and was a full time college student. I looked around, but it was useless. I offered my cousin all my student loan money, my child support money and my financial aid money so that she would allow me to live with her for a while so that I can continue to go to school. She agreed to let me stay and we decided to do this.

I knew it would be very challenging for me because like I said, her house was in dire need of a full-time maid and she didn't hire one. She had used a cleaning couple to clean the house from time to time, but by the time I moved in, those two had stopped working in there. Also, there was constant chaos in this house because of her mentally disabled brothers who both have a criminal record of domestic violence and other things. I had to figure out a way to pass all my classes, keep the house decent so my son and I can be mentally stable, and I had to figure out how to do all that in the middle of utter chaos and disarray. I also had to figure out a way to do all those things, without giving up my time in prayer, fasting and the study of Scriptures. That was a great mountain for me to climb!

Shortly after I moved in there, I graduated from Miami Dade College with an Associates Degree in Psychology. I was so happy! This was by far, one of my happiest moment in life since I had gotten sick in 1996. I couldn't believe that I finally graduated! God is the One to truly get the glory for this achievement. Had it not been for Him softening the hearts of my past land lords and allowing me to go more than four months without paying them my rent, without them kicking me out, I would have not made it. If He had not allowed me to drive to school day in and day out without my car insurance, with an expired license tag and with my driver's license suspended from time to time, without me getting locked up for it, I would have not made it either!

If He had not protected me and given me the victory for all the times I was taken to court to fight for my son's custody, I would have not made it. If He had not made a supernatural miracle and messed around with the Miami Dade College computers when I tried to register for the first time after owing them more than $600, I would not have even been able to start school before first paying them what I owed. If He would have not allowed me to qualify for all the loans and the financial aid that I got, I would have not made it either.

If He would not have strengthened me when I broke up with my atheist boyfriend, when I was evicted over and over, or when I went through the trial with my brother and Hailie's mom, when I had to take care of Hailie and my son without much help, when I lost Hailie and when my grandmother died, I would have collapsed! If He had not been there for me when I had to live with my son's father again, and be set up by him to lose everything, or the time when I had to live with my cousin Andrew and find out I was raped by five guys, and then also be set up to lose everything again because of me investing myself in helping him, I would have not made it! Truly the easy part was studying and passing the exams and my classes and that was as hard as can be! However, He took care of the parts that were not only hard, but impossible for me to achieve on my own. I owe Him my degree!

Furthermore, during these days, I was attending my church: "King Jesus Ministries." I was still going to their school of ministers and taking one or two classes every Monday night. I was only going to those classes and to some services. I had been focusing hard on my college classes and surviving all the trials I just mentioned I was going through. I had been spending a lot of time with the prophetess that had taken me with her to Peru for my liberation. She had been mentoring me in many new things that I did not know. She really opened my eyes to new revelations of the Spirit. She took me to a couple of different prophetic churches. In one of those churches, she told me that she had seen my "husband." I did not understand what she was talking about. She said that she saw a man that she just knew that he was my husband, but that she also knew that even though he was the man of God, that God had for me, he was not ready, because he was in love with another woman. As confusing as that was for me, I was still curious to see what she was talking to me about and of course, I visited this new church with her, and saw the man. I ended up meeting him and we spoke a little bit.

We got to know each other by phone, and he was very prophetic and anointed. I was super excited about him, but also very confused and disturbed in my spirit, because indeed he was involved with another woman. He told me they had been dating on and off, for a while, and that he knew she was not really the woman of God for him, yet, they were still on and off. I was very attracted to him and hoped that he was indeed the husband that God had for me. I had stayed single for a very long time and prayed a lot for God to bring me someone that would help me be more holy and closer to Him. I had faith that even though he was on and off with this woman, that somehow it would work out for the best in God's holy and perfect will.

We became friends, but we saw each other very little. Our friendship was more by phone. Moreover, as the days went by, things in Scarlett's house just got harder and harder with each passing day. I had worked really hard in keeping the living room floor without dog pee, and dog poop, by picking it up and cleaning it, and by mopping the floor over and over, and by restlessly walking the three of them three times a day. I was exhausted from all that labor, but I felt an inner sense of pride that I finally had the house clean and the dogs were well groomed and trained. Furthermore, just when I thought that I had this under control, Scarlett brought home a two-year-old boxer dog. Even though, I thought the dog was majestically beautiful, when I saw her standing in the middle of the living room that I had just finished mopping for hours, and when I saw her squat down and pee what looked like a lake in our living room, I just wanted to throw myself down on the floor and cry!

I could not believe what was happening! I thought this was Satan playing his cards to check mate me. I was already super tired from all the cleaning and the picking up the pee and poop, I was exhausted from walking them daily three times a day and from having to bathe them one by one, and then blow dry their hair, I couldn't imagine adding another dog into the whole ordeal, and another small dog would have been terrible, but this was not even a small dog, this was a huge dog, and a very strong and hyper one too! I was devastated!

But how I felt and what I thought about this did not matter! Scarlett was the owner of the house, she was the one who paid the main bills and I was a nobody in there, who was just there by her mercy toward me, so I had to "submit" to whatever she did and desired and suck it up!

When the boxer got home, the other smaller dogs didn't like her at all. They used to bark at her for a long time and she was just a puppy and would get scared and I would see her trying to hide from them in a corner. It was very loud and noisy having all these dogs barking all the time at the boxer. I had to start walking the boxer and then the other three dogs. So now my walking the dog's routine doubled up on me. I also ended up having to bathe the boxer and of course, I was the one cleaning most of her pee and poop in the house.

In the meantime, I was also having to help my son do his homework everyday after he came back from school.

And sometimes he would give me a real hard time because he did not want to do it. I also had to help my cousin's son do his work, when my cousin was out working and my cousin's best friend who has eight children, used to come to her house every day after school with most of her children and they would all sit down in the table to do their homework. Between the dogs and the children in the house, I had plenty of work to do and plenty of noise to endure.

But let's not forget that my whole financial life depended on me going through college. After I graduated from Miami Dade College, I immediately registered into Liberty University Online. Since I had good grades, I qualified for a $30,000 scholarship to go to this school. I wanted to study at home so I can take good care of my son after school and not have to worry about having to figure out a way to go to school with him being taken care of. I was super excited that I qualified for all that money and that it was totally possible for me to go through school without work and help Scarlett out with money from school, for renting her room. But I had to study while at the same time I had to deal with the dogs, cats, birds and every animal that was in there and their mess! I had to deal with all the kitchen mess that everyone in the house would leave for me to clean, I had to deal with all the noise and traffic of adults and children that was constantly going through the house, and I had to deal with the amount of time lost just in walking and bathing all the four dogs, and then I had to deal with my son and all the time homework would take him.

Yet with much prayer and pleading the blood of Jesus Christ over my life, I was surviving it. However, Satan wasn't done in hitting me with his best shots, thus, he threw me a curve ball that I had not seen coming. My cousin Andrew and his wife moved in with us. This was Satan's check mate for me, and my Online school would certainly go down the drain! No matter how disciplined I would be in doing my school work to pass my classes, all that doesn't matter when you have two adults in the house screaming all kinds of vulgar names at each other and throwing crystal candles toward their foreheads, as if they were a baseball player throwing a ball when he is pitching it to the player standing with a bat, breaking the skin wide open and causing blood to splatter out upon the walls, the floor and the furniture like in a horror movie.

These two people would bring the dogs, the cats, the kids and me to our knees! They were just so scary in the way they would fight. I don't even know how they didn't kill each other. Andrew's wife had two children from a previous marriage and during these apocalyptic fights that they would have, I was the one having to hide in the rooms and bathrooms with Scarlett's son, my son and Andrew's two step children; we hid together with all the dogs who were just as frightened as we all were. I remember we would all be praying to God for the fighting to stop. Scarlett was usually never home. She was working most of the time! Lucky her! She got to skip all that drama!

I was only able to last my first semester in Liberty University. I could not study in the middle of so much chaos and labor. I now was in big trouble thou, because school was my financial method to pay my rent and I didn't have that anymore. As if that wasn't challenging enough, my car broke down for good once again. So I was carless and with no money. I was literally trapped in my cousin's house once again. I had a pattern where I would get trapped in people's houses and with no choice but to wait on God to intervene and rescue me out.

Well, now that my income from school is gone, all hell broke loose against me. Everyone in the house started to hate on me. But that was not the worst part, they began hating and bullying my son. I was pinned down unto a wall and had no way to properly protect my son from them because I couldn't leave the house and they had total ruler-ship over us since we didn't have any money. I truly entered into a nightmare very similar to the fairytale of Cinderella. I ended up becoming that full time maid that the house was in dire need of, but no one appreciated anything of what I did for them, nor did I get paid for what I did, even though there are many people who make a nice living doing the same things I did in that home and perhaps working even less. They all acted as if I was just a leach, who was tak-ing advantage of Scarlett and being a burden to her. Even though her son was being taken care of by me while she was out working. She ended up moving her mother and Johnny out of our house for an entire two years, and all that time, the only person attending her son while she worked dou-ble shifts, was me. I walked him and my son to school in the mornings and walked them back home after school. I helped them both do their homework, I cooked meals for them, cleaned up after them, kept them entertained, took them outside to play, read to them, taught them the Bible, prayed for them, etc. But in everyone's eyes, I was an irresponsible, lazy leach, taking advantage of my hard, working cousin.

Thus, my cousin wanted me to find me a job. I also wanted to find me a job. But the problem was that I didn't have anyone sane to leave my child with. My cousin didn't have a problem leaving her son alone with my son. But God had a problem with that and so did I. She also didn't have a problem leaving her son and my son alone with her crazy and mentally ill brothers. But God had a problem with that and so did I. Thus, everyone in the house began punishing me for having an issue about leaving our underage children alone or with mentally ill and abusive people. All that didn't matter to any of them, everyone expected for me to not care about that and to abandon the children to go to work. They began to manifest their anger toward me by bullying my son and me. We were tested in this house beyond the wildest imaginations. To make a long story short, I ended up going to the emergency room a couple of times, with symptoms of a heart attack. Between all the physical labor I was subjected to and all the stress from everyone hating on my son and me, I almost had a heart attack. By the grace of God, I didn't have one.

My son had a meltdown as well in his school. The school staff called me and let me know that my son was screaming and crying in the middle of his class and claiming that the only ones who loved him were his parents, but that everyone else hated him. They wanted me to put him in therapy, but I knew that the first thing the therapist would do was to put him under horrible medications that only make him worse. So I asked them to please give me some time to work on him and that I knew he would get better. They did. And after time passed, in the middle of the situation we were in, with much prayer, fasting, interceding and time with my son and God alone, my son not only got better, he won an award in school for best turned around child. This is an award granted to one child per school in the District that was having some sort of emotional or behavioral problems, but then they became good and stable.

Meanwhile, as I was juggling with having to deal with my son's depression, the full time job of having to maintain a farm in the middle of a house, the emotional strength that it took to deal with all the rage, wrath and jealousy that came from all those people in the home toward me, I decided to try to get jobs cleaning other people's home while the kids were in school. I passed out flyers and actually got a couple of jobs and paid my cousin with all the money I would earn, except my tithes. I would still, continue to pay my tithes from whatever money I would get. During these days of passing out flyers to clean homes I got a proposition from a man to marry him for papers and he offered me a great amount of money. I declined the offer. Marriage is something very sacred and I would never play around with something like that. No money in the world is worth lying about marriage. Also, liars will have their part in the lake of fire. I plan to not end up there.

But the fearful, and unbelieving, and the abominable, and murderers, and whoremongers, and sorcerers, and idolaters, and all liars, shall have their part in the lake which burneth with

fire and brimstone: which is the second death. Revelation 21:8

I also got a phone call from someone offering me a program for people who were disable or mentally ill, she told me that since I had once been diagnosed with schizophrenia, that I would totally qualify. She told me it is a program where they would pay for me to be able to go to school and help me pay rent and buy food and even pay for transportation. All I had to do was apply and show them my medical records. But I also declined. Because I am healed from Schizophrenia and by the power of God, I am no longer mentally ill or disabled. I was not going to curse myself with the demons of Schizophrenia for money. No way! I declined this proposition without a second thought to it. I would rather be poor and homeless than to undue the marvelous work of Jesus Christ in my life and mind by declaring that I am still mentally ill.

Moreover, even though, I wasn't getting money from school anymore, I was still getting some child support, even though from time to time, the child support would stop coming. I was still getting money from friends from church that would donate money to me, and I was earning money cleaning houses, but I didn't get too many calls for me to work cleaning houses. Only a few houses, I made $100 per house, because they were very big. I always gave my cousin most of the money, after paying my tithes. I also gave her the student loans I first got which were thousands of dollars that I still owe to this day.

I came to a point that I was in so much agony, in so much need of money, and just so tired of the humiliation and exploitation that I was experiencing, that I actually contemplated to go ahead and take a job outside of the home and leave the kids alone or with the abusers of the house, but instantly, God gave me a dream. This was the dream: Jesus was holding in His arms Scarlett's son and He was approaching me while holding the child in His arms. As He gets close to me, He tells me: "Desiree, if you take care of this child, you will have a crown waiting for you in heaven for doing this"... I then replied back to Jesus: "Yes, Jesus, I will do it, I will take care of him!" And so Jesus handed me over the child and as I grabbed the child in my arms, I heard my sister in the background screaming at me: "NO! You need to go out to work, forget about that and go get a job!" But I ignored her voice and just kept on walking with my new assignment from heaven in my arms. Thus, the moral of this story is that going out and working is not always what is most important to Jesus, sometimes the lives of His most vulnerable children is what is most important.

Another night, I had a dream where I was sitting down with my earthly father, whom passed away in real life. I was crying and weeping upon his lap, and I was telling him that I just wanted to get me a real job, I was telling him that I just wanted to be like everyone else. I wanted to earn my own money and be independent, but then my father replied with much compassion in his voice: "Desi, I know that you want to work and earn your own money and be like everyone else, but you can't because you are a LEVITE!"

When I woke up that morning, I had no idea what Levites were, so I looked it up in the Bible and it turned out to be the most amazing revelation ever... I learned that those were the people that were consecrated for God's service and that they were to be completely separated from the secular lifestyle and focus on only serving in the tabernacle of God. These were the people of God who were entitled to receive tithes and offerings from the people they served, and they were prohibited to work in secular jobs or to have the same heritage as the Israelites. These people were to be dependent on God and God was their heritage.

And the Lord spake unto Aaron, Thou shalt have no inheritance in their land, neither shalt thou have any part among them: I am thy part and thine inheritance among the children of Israel. And, behold, I have given the children of Levi all the tenth in Israel for an inheritance, for their service which they serve, even the service of the tabernacle of the congregation. Numbers 18:20-21

As a result of these dreams, I now was affirmed in much conviction from the Lord, that no matter what they would do to me in this home, I was to stay in there and work for God and take good care of the kids. Throughout this whole nightmare, I had stopped hearing from the guy that I thought was my husband to be. The last thing he told me was to wait for him. He wanted to end things with that other woman the right way and respectfully. He said to write to him by email if I desired to do so, but that he was going to be away for a while. So I did that. I wrote to him. I wrote my heart out to him for years. And if it had not been for those emails, I truly don't think I would have endured the entire process at my cousin's house. He didn't reply to me. I would ask him to tell me if he wanted me to stop writing to him and if he had decided to move on without me, and that I would stop writing because it felt strange to me to write so much without his reply. But he didn't tell me to stop writing either. And here is the mystery of this whole ordeal. God began giving me prophetic dreams about him and I would write them to him. He began showing me things about his life and I would tell him in the emails the things I was shown. I began dreaming of him daily. Then, I would write daily what I dreamt. I began to also get prophetic dreams about other people and the people would tell me that my dreams about them were right.

Thus, I began to feel convicted that what I was dreaming about this guy was also true, even though I wasn't getting any feedback from him, because he was not responding to me. However, I got tired of writing to him without any reply and I was going to quit writing to him, but then God in dreams would ordain me to keep writing to him. Thus, I would obey God and continue telling him everything. I wrote him all my prophetic dreams and revelations, I wrote to him all the nightmare I was enduring in the house I was in, I wrote to him prayers for his life and many teachings of the word of God that the Lord was showing me. This time of writing to him became my therapy. I felt strengthened by God through this exercise. But I also fell in love, head over hills in love with my mystery cyber boyfriend who would not reply to me for years now.

One day, after years of not receiving not even a single email from him, I finally received an email from him.

However, there was nothing that he wrote on it. He sent me an article about a job that was done in the home from the computer and that many stay at home moms were doing to get by. I was super happy and confused at the same time. Finally, I know for sure he has been reading my emails and that I am not crazy and writing to a ghost. But then, he only sends me a job offer. Nothing else. And even though the job seemed great, the Lord didn't want me working on anything other than what I was already doing. I had no time for any other extra activity, and He made that very clear to me through many prophetic dreams that He gave me. He wanted me cleaning the home, keeping the animals in check and well groomed, cooking for everyone, taking good care of the kids, praying and reading the Bible and serving the Lord. Which I was serving the Lord, with other people. As I was going through all the war in my cousin's house, I was also preaching and helping other people outside my family and house and they were getting the very best of my service.

By this time, I was only attending my church when there was no one in there. I was there praying my heart out to God. Being in my cousin's house was one of the hardest times of my entire life and truly my only escape was spending time alone in the church I used to go to. I thank God for that church and will forever be grateful they had that Oasis for me to go to during my darkest years in life.

CHAPTER 14

MEETING MY TRUE HUSBAND

One morning in the year 2011, I woke up from a dream and as I usually did, I went to my computer and wrote the entire dream to my mystery boyfriend and emailed it to him. By now, I had already been writing to him since we met in 2010. I thought that he was my husband to be and that I was to wait patiently for him to return to me when he was ready by God to do so. The reason for my conviction about him was mainly because of all the dreams that I had been getting about him. So this morning, the dream I wrote to him was this: I was with him in a boat. It was a lovely, sunny day. I could see the skies above us as we sailed the ocean in this nice boat, it was blue and clear. In the dream we were a couple. I was very happy with him in this boat. As we were happily cruising around in the middle of the ocean, I suddenly see that the skies began to change. Really big, dark clouds began to approach and started to dim out the sunlight. Then the wind began to blow much more rapidly, and it was rocking the boat back and forth as well as the waters below us. It was a huge storm that had unfolded in a matter of seconds. I looked at my boyfriend and I can see in his face that he was really scared. He was the one driving the boat. I was leaning by the side of the boat and noticed that I was now holding on to my journal, which in real life I used to write my life story in it. I was embracing my journal hard as if trying to protect it from getting wet by the rain that now began falling upon us and the waves of the ocean that was starting to sneak inside the boat.

I felt really scared too and I didn't understand what was going on? As I was trying to ponder on what we were experiencing, I noticed that my boyfriend came toward me out of fear and began to try to kiss me. But in the dream, I had to stop him from kissing me because it was going to cause my journal, (which had the story of my life inside of it) to get wet and ruined. Thus, I stopped him, and I knew that the right thing to do was to stop and protect the journal/book.

When I wrote to him this dream, I told him that I believed that this was a prophetic warning from God to tell us to guard our hearts and not sin sexually with anyone. I told him that I believed that for the sake of my story/testimony we both needed to stay away from sexual sin between each other or with other people.

A couple of days later, I was really stressed out in my house. It was the afternoon and I could no longer stand the feeling I had inside. I was so frustrated about my life. I hated the life I had. I was tired of being "Cinderella." I was tired of being single. I was tired of being rejected by everyone and unappreciated. I was tired of cleaning so much and never keeping the house clean for long because of the many animals and people in the house. I was tired of writing to my boyfriend in emails and never hearing back from him. I was tired of not being able to provide for my son a better life and I was tired of having him around people that were not good role models at all and were purposely hurting him. I wanted to be free. I wanted to have a change. I needed to pray and pray hard. Thus, that day I decided to go to church during the afternoon. My church was near my place and they used to keep the temple open so that anyone who wished to go pray, they can. I was hoping that when I got in there, no one would be there. I was hoping to spend some good quality time alone with God and pray for God to finally bring me my husband. I wanted my husband from God to be with me more than anything else. I had been single for many years by now and I was tired of having that lifestyle. Being single isn't so bad when you don't have any children, but being a single mom, without my parents or family to help me, is the hardest thing I have ever endured.

Furthermore, I entered the doors of the church and was ready to pour out my heart to God in worship, when suddenly I noticed this man sitting down on a chair right on front of the altar. I was upset at his presence there, because I really wanted to be alone. But I was so desperate, that I chose to ignore him. I went right on front of him and stood up on front of the altar and raised up my hands and began to worship God out loud. I didn't care if he thought I was crazy or sang bad or anything. I was so tired inside of myself, so sad, so frustrated, that if I didn't do that, I was going to explode!

I sang for a while and then I went on my knees and began to pray. I was asking God to please have mercy on me and to send me my husband. I was begging him to convict him to reply to my emails or that if God Himself was telling him to not respond my emails, to stop it, and to give him permission to talk back to me. I was telling Him I didn't want to wait anymore for a husband. As I was telling God all these things, as I was bowing down on the floor, I felt a hand tap me on my arm. I looked to my side and see that it was the man that had been sitting there when I first got there. I had even forgotten that someone was in the church with me. I looked up and see him looking down to me. Then I hear the words: "Would you mind praying for me please?"

For an instance, I felt annoyed. Here I was in dire need of prayer myself, and this stranger came and interrupted me to have me pray for him. But quickly the Lord moved my spirit to have compassion over him and forget about myself. Thus, I asked him what he wished me to pray for and he told me that he had just found out his girlfriend of five years and the mother of his youngest child had been having an affair. He was devastated! I can feel his pain as he began telling me what was happening. He told me that he was having wicked thoughts about retaliating against them and that he needed prayer to stop those evil thoughts because he didn't really want to do anything crazy. I began praying for him. After I prayed, I heard the Spirit of God ordaining me to give him my phone number. I usually never give out my phone number, not even to women. But I knew that God was asking me to give him my number and to help him out. So I did!

I went back home after we spoke for a while and then he called me. He told me that after he found out that she was cheating on him, they got into a huge fight and she kicked him out of their place. He was now in the streets with nowhere to go. He didn't know what to do. He was really in great pain. I talked to him about God through the phone and tried to spend time consoling him. He slept in his car for a couple of days and I would spend time with him during the day time and evenings in his car to accompany him. He ended up renting a small efficiency and I would bring him food because he was short of money. I wrote a bunch of verses of the Bible in black letters, on bright colored typing paper and pasted them all over his efficiency. I wanted him to wake up and the first thing that he would see would be the word of God. I wanted him to see the word of God right before going to sleep. This was something I did with my own room when I first got saved and it worked! We became friends. But in my mind, he was someone that I was ordained by God to help in a dark time of his life. This man would not have been the first man that God would ordain me to help this way. I had already done this with many different people, both men and women. As time kept passing by, he began telling me that I was his wife. He said he had prophets tell him that I was his wife that God had for him. I looked at him as if he was crazy! There is no way that is true, because I just knew without a shadow of a doubt that my online, mystery boyfriend was the man that God wanted for me. I told him that I had many prophets get it wrong concerning my spouse. I told him that they had prophesied to me the same thing with my exes and that here I was, without them. I told him that he needed to know that they were wrong.

I never meant to hurt him, I was just convinced that they were truly lying or deceived about that. I was sure that it was not him. Although, he was not happy about that, he didn't care. He continued to spend time with me, and I continued to disciple him in the Lord. I was taking my sweet time to teach him about the spiritual battle we are in. I got books about spiritual warfare and would sit in his car for hours and read them to him. I also read the Bible to him and prayed over his life repeatedly.

As time went by, I noticed that he had a very short temper. I noticed that whenever he disagreed with me concerning the things I would speak to him about God and His word, he would snap at me in rage. I began to feel a little weary every time we would sit down and debate the word of God. He used a lot of foul language and I didn't like that at all. I had conquered my tongue and it took me many years and much hard work for me to stop cursing and I didn't want to be around people who cursed. Even though everyone in the house we lived in cursed like crazy. But I had no choice when it came to those people. But with this guy, I did. So after thinking about it for a long time, I felt that I just simply had too many problems in my own life to help him. I thought that I just didn't have the strength to deal with someone like him that would get so angry so easily and so fast. I even nick named him: "Fosforito" which means little match, as of (fire) in Spanish.

I also was feeling a little tempted by him sexually. He insisted in trying to flirt with me and I was just not wanting to fall into any sexual temptation at all. I kept remembering the dream I had just had and shared with my online boyfriend. I now knew that the dream was my warning concerning this guy, Richard. Every time he would flirt with me, I would shiver with fear. I was terrified to fall into sexual sin with him and betray God and my online boyfriend. I also feared messing up my book that I was writing by doing the wrong things. Thus, after much thinking I decided to cut off my friendship with Richard. I told him by phone that I was very sorry, but that I could not continue to be his friend or to pray for him and teach him the Bible or to go to church together. I told him that I needed to focus on getting my own life in order and that it was just best if we stopped seen each other. I explained to him I also didn't want to sin with him sexually. So he received my words and that was the end of it. So I thought!

That very same night, after I cut it all off and was very determined and dead serious in never talking to Richard again, I had a dream. In this dream, I was in an Airport. I was standing in the middle of the Airport with a brown dog. It was a middle size, brown dog. I was bathing the dog and the dog was full of soap. I was scrubbing him really hard with soap and I could see a lot of mud and dirt just coming down with the soap. Then I moved away from him for a moment to grab the hose and right when I was about to hose him down with water, the dog began to get scared of the hose and ran away from me. I was terrified when the dog left and frantically began screaming out his name: "Richard!" "Richard!" Richard!" Come back please! Richard! Richard! I ran and ran after the dog, but I lost him. I was deeply saddened and scared for him. I looked at the hallways of the Airport and all of them were empty and he was nowhere to be seen.

When I woke up, the Holy Spirit told me that if I cut off my relationship with Richard he would get lost forever. He said that the dog in the dream represented him and that the soap and water represented the word of God that I was teaching Him. He ordained me to call him back and to continue to disciple him in His ways and to be patient with his temper. So I did!

I called him back and told him all about my dream and so we were back. We hung out everywhere. We went to church together, we picked up his daughter and took her and my son to all these cool places where they would have fun together. It was nice for me, because I barely went anywhere ever. I never had any money to do anything like that. I went with him to my sister's Thanksgiving dinners and we would go out to eat at restaurants and he just gave me a break from my every day boring routine as well. We were each other's comfort. Richard told me about the time that we met in the church, how when he first got in there, he had been praying about what had just happened between him and his ex-girlfriend and he said to me that he had been asking God to give him a good woman that would truly love him and be with him. Then he told me that right after he said that prayer, I entered the church. When I first heard this, I was as disturbed as when he told me that they told him that I was his wife. I just didn't want to hear that, because that meant I was all wrong about my online boyfriend and that all those prophetic dreams about us being a couple were all wrong and thus, that was just too confusing for me to process. How could I be so wrong about those dreams, but at the same time have many other prophetic dreams about other people and they confirm to me that I was right? It just didn't make any sense. So my only conclusion was that Richard was wrong about me being his wife and that the prayer that he said and my walking into his life right after was just one big coincidence. There is just no other explanation.

However, I couldn't stop the feeling of love that I was starting to feel toward him by now and I couldn't deny that I truly enjoyed his company. I couldn't understand why God didn't let me separate from him and ordained me to help him instead. However, from time to time, his bad temper would wake me up from my vacation with him and make me wonder if I should stay away from him. But when I would find myself contemplating leaving him, I would be reminded of my dream with the brown dog in the Airport and thus, I would rebuke those thoughts and continued to hang out with him and talk to him.

However, as much as we liked each other's company and enjoyed each other, I had my online boyfriend on my mind the entire time. I would still be writing to him emails daily. I would tell him everything. I told him about Richard and about how we met and even my dream with the dog in the Airport. I was also driving Richard crazy, because I would not stop talking about my online boyfriend. I would keep drilling in his head that he was my husband and that we just weren't supposed to be together yet because God was pruning both of us so that we may be mature enough to work out a good relationship when we do get together. I genuinely believed all that with all my heart. There were way too many prophetic dreams that God had given me to make me believe that. There was nothing and no one that could change my mind about that. I was convinced!

This of course, bothered Richard greatly, but he endured it. He had no other choice but to endure it or just break off our friendship. As time kept passing by, Richard and I began to get too close to each other. I was starting to have strong feelings toward him, and he was also starting to cause me to stumble in sexual sin. I now didn't think about the dream of the dog anymore, I decided to cut off our relationship because I felt he was going to cause me to fall into sexual sin and get all those demons that were once inside of me back in me and stronger. I was terrified at the thought of that or at the thought of dying in my sin. So I left him!

I worked hard at forgetting about Richard, even though I missed him dearly. I fought my flesh with all my might and just focused on getting back to how I used to be, before meeting him. I continued writing emails to my online boyfriend and having faith that he would soon answer me back. Richard would show up to my house every so often and I would hide from him. He would talk with my cousin and then leave. Time passed and one day he called me letting me know that his brother was found dead in a hotel room after he hung himself. I felt bad for him and I decided to accompany him to his brother's funeral. I spent the entire night with him in the funeral home and then he dropped me off back home.

We became friends again, but I still had my distance with him. I still was waiting on my "husband" from God and it wasn't him. I tried hard to stay far away from Richard because I didn't want to sin sexually. Things in my cousin's house were also such a trial for me that I could not afford to give Satan any legal right to attack me, because he was already tormenting me to the fullest! I had to live in pure holiness and obedience to God if I intended to live! I was surrounded by wolves and they were salivating at my life and my son's life daily, hovering over both us and looking how to enter in and eat us alive! It wasn't only my cousins who were bullying my son and I, it was also my cousin's friends and neighbors who would be there all the time and spent endless hours gossiping about me and playing hoaxes against us.

I also had been helping a man who had been a Satanist for over twenty years to get to know the Lord. I had been working with this man on and off and I knew that if I was going to venture and to dare to disciple someone of that level, that I needed to be holy! Sin had no place in my life, or I would be dead! Literally dead!

Thus, once again I separated from Richard and was back to my old self. But years had passed by and my cousin was very tired of having me in her home. I was also very tired of living there, but God did not want to move me out and He also had prohibited me from getting me a job. I remember when I first moved in my cousin's house, a young lady from the last church I attended prophesied to me that she saw that the Lord was not going to move me out of the place I was in until I put that place in order. This young lady had no idea who I was or where I lived. Then her mother preached a sermon and before she began preaching it, she told me that the message was for me. It was a message about how God sometimes will place us in a creek to save the souls that live in there. Sometimes He will make us be in horrible places for the love of those people who abide in there. My job was to put that crazy house in order, both spiritually and physically. My job was to educate and protect all the children that were in that house and to not allow anything bad to happen to them, to the best of my ability, I was to protect them.

Unfortunately, they still were able to hurt my son a lot. One day, while I was cleaning the bathroom upstairs, the adults and children in the house bullied my son without me knowing and traumatized him to the max! I remember he came to me crying hysterically and screaming that he hated them all and I just could not find out from him what was it that they did to him. I went downstairs and told them off, but of course is a joke to all of them, since I was no one in their eyes, I was just one big loser. Years later, when my son was older, he explained to me that they pulled down his pants and laughed at him, they hosed him down with the hose and they even shot him with a BB gun and all of them just laughed at him. I could not believe it! What is wrong with all them? They should be arrested for child abuse!

Scarlett was one of the ones who laughed at him and did not protect him, while I was always caring for her son with the best service to be given. When my son told me all this, I almost fainted! I was utterly devastated! I cried for days! And even though I was greatly upset at all of them, I forgave them. I had to! If this is what they would do while I was just cleaning the bathroom, imagine what things they would have done unto him, if I had been outside of the home, in a secular job for eight hours a day? Another method of torture that they would use against my son, was to gossip major nasty things about me on front of him, while I was upstairs, and he was downstairs with them. It became so bad, that my son had to stay with me in the room most of the time. We were like in a prison and we became cell mates in our room.

Things had gotten so bad at my cousin's house, that I decided that my son was better off moving out and living with his dad. I thought that maybe I would be a better mother to my son if I gave him up to his dad. I needed to make sure I was making my decision concerning his best interest and even though I had no idea of just how bad my son was being treated by all these people we lived with, I knew that he was being mistreated to a certain degree and that he was also suffering by simply watching them mistreat me and constantly speak bad about me to my face and behind my back on front of him. I asked his father to take him in and his father took him, because he was a little bit older now, and he planned to leave him alone in his apartment while he worked. However, he was still in Elementary school, and in my opinion that is still too young for him to stay home alone, but I could not think he was better off with the people we lived with either. I prayed and said to God that if that was what was best for my son, so be it. I told him that I would give him my son the same way that Abraham gave him Isaac. I didn't want to make an idol of my son either in my life, nor did I want to selfishly keep him with me, knowing that he was suffering. So the day my son left to his father' s house, the Spirit of God told me that in two weeks he will be back with me.

And it came to pass after these things, that God did tempt (test) Abraham, and said unto him, Abraham: and he said, Behold, here I am. And he

said, Take now thy son, thine only son Isaac, whom thou lovest, and get thee into the land of Moriah; and offer him there for a burnt offering upon one of the mountains which I will tell thee of. Genesis 22:1-2

And the angel of the Lord called unto him out of heaven, and said, Abraham, Abraham: and he said, Here am I. And he said, Lay not thine hand upon the lad, neither do thou any thing unto him: for now I know that thou fearest God, seeing thou hast not with-held thy son, thine only son from me. Genesis 22:11-12

Exactly two weeks later, my son called me crying from his father's house telling me that he wanted to come back to live with me. He said he didn't like living in his father's house at all and that he felt lonely and scared because his father worked a lot and he was left home alone a lot. He shared with me a scary experience he had one day while home alone, he said he got tempted to look at women in the computer and then he got on his knees and prayed, but he felt a lot of fear creep up within him and it was so bad, that he became afraid of praying after that event. When my son shared this with me, the Lord spoke to me about this. The Lord told me that this is the reason why the devil took women out of the homes and into the working place. Women were meant to be the spiritual coverings of their children, thus, when children are home alone, there is no spiritual protection over them. The men are the spiritual covering of the wife and children, but the women become the spiritual covering of the children while the men are out of the home. This is exactly what happened to Ted Bundy, the famous serial killer who was executed. He was left home alone at the age of twelve years old and watched pornography and violent films and became a monster.

Thus, my son moved in right back with me. Even though I was relieved that he was back home with me and those two weeks were probably the hardest days in my cousin's house for me, I was once again super stressed out and scared of having my baby in the midst of so many hateful people. It was a warzone!

The time came that my cousin decided to legally evict me. I asked God if I should move out to my sister's house after my sister offered to have me go with her and God told me no. He instructed me to just allow them to kick me out. He asked me to have faith and to trust Him and that everything I was going to go through was under His control. At first, I naively thought He was going to do a supernatural miracle and out of nowhere provide for me my own place. Why not? I had prayed and fasted enough about it, I had been working my heart out in this house for four years and submitted to very hard labor and mistreatment. I had stayed obedient in paying my tithes to Him through it all and stuck with the process. Thus, I thought He might be up to something and was going to surprise me. But unfortunately, what He was actually asking me to do was to become homeless for Him. I did! My cousin evicted me, and I then became homeless.

Even though I could not understand why God was asking me to do this, I trusted Him and obeyed Him. Even though I was terrified of what was going to happen to me and my son, I trusted Him and allowed Him to do His will in our lives.

CHAPTER 15

HOMELESS

The police came to my cousin's house and kicked me out. My son was supposed to go with his father and his father came to pick him up, but when the moment came for him to separate from me, my son began crying and crying and he also became angry and told his father he didn't want to go with him. It was so bad and so painful for his father to see his son this way, that he brought him back to me and told me that he could not take him this way. I told my son that even though I did not know where I was going, I would never tell him to not come with me. He can choose to be with me if that is what he wanted to do. I always had faith that God was in control of everything going on and I also knew that it would be the will of God for my son to go with his father or to stay with me. Thus, his father left, and my son stayed with me.

It turned out, that what the enemy used to try to destroy me, was what God ended up using to take me through the whole situation I was in. Prior to my eviction moment, my cousin and my son's father had called the social service people on me to investigate me, because they were claiming that I was not fit to have custody of my son. They were trying to frame me as if I was mentally ill and that was the reason why I didn't want to go out and work and provide for my son and me. When the lady interviewed me, I explained to her that the reason why I could not get a job was because I did not have anyone safe to leave my underage child with and I also explained to her that my cousin was peer pressuring me into leaving him and her underage son alone, or with her crazy, mentally ill, drug addicted and domestic violent brothers, whom one of them was being accused of doing really bad things to his step children and had even been to jail with some serious charges concerning the kids and his wife. The social worker then took my cousin's son apart and interviewed him and she confirmed that he was indeed being left home alone plenty of times when I didn't live with him and that he was also being left home alone with his crazy uncles. The social worker then got in my side and she arranged for me to go to this homeless program that they had. She made a bunch of calls and even fought for me to get a decent place to stay in, I was impressed by this woman's determination to help me out and deeply grateful that she was moved with compassion to do all the things she did for me, which I knew she really didn't have to do them. They ended up taking me and my son to a Motel that was paid by them.

Before I was evicted, the social service department made me go through a psychological evaluation to confirm if I was still crazy and I passed their tests as someone who is sound minded. During this entire nightmare, I began a ministry in Facebook that the Lord had ordained me to start. I had never been in FB before. I had tried to get in it in 2010 but the Lord ordained me to stay away from it. Then in 2014, after He gave me dreams about tsunamis and judgments coming upon the USA, He ordained me to get in FB and warn the people. Thus, as I was getting evicted, I was starting to warn the people of all the dreams and visions and prophetic words of judgment that was to come upon America. I had also transferred my son from his school to homeschool. I didn't really know what was going to happen to us, but I intended to keep him learning as much as possible. I registered him in a Christian online homeschool program and I was helping him to take those classes.

I was extremely sad, extremely humiliated, extremely hurt, extremely tired, but at the same time, I never stopped tithing, I never stopped taking good care of my son and I never stopped the ministry in FB. When we left my cousin's house and rode off to the Motel, even though we were torn apart, my son and I felt a huge relief that we were finally out of that house. We were actually smiling on our way out. We stayed in this Motel for four months. We got there by the end of October. On the morning after Halloween night, I opened the door and I noticed feathers all over my door and on the floor on front of the door. I knew that it was witchcraft. That night I actually became really ill out of nowhere. I was scared to death. I didn't have a car and I had no idea what would happen to my son alone if something was to happen to me. Thankfully, I prayed throughout my high fever and the next day I got better.

My son and I would pray together every single day and take the holy communion every single night before going to sleep. He began to hear the voice of the Lord and he also started to get prophetic dreams. One of the nights in that Motel, my son had a dream where he was in a Fema Camp type of place and he was making a line along with many other kids and they were having to choose to take the mark of the beast on their bodies or to be killed. My son said that he saw some of his friends taking the mark of the beast, but that he chose to be killed and then he said that after they chopped off his head in a guillotine, he went to heaven and that he was with me and that we were having a lot of fun. He said we were skiing in snow and that he was playing all kinds of sports. I believe the Lord is preparing my son for what is to come through those dreams.

And it shall come to pass in the last days, saith God, I will pour out of my Spirit upon all flesh: and your sons and your daughters shall prophesy, and your young men shall see visions, and your old men shall dream dreams. Acts 2:17

Meanwhile, I was warning and warning a lot of people in FB about the things to come. I was also revealing a lot of truth and exposing a lot of lies and teaching the word of God and things that the Lord has taught me. I spent hours and hours working in FB and it took a lot of energy and time from me. I friended a lot of celebrities and many of them let me in, but a lot of them would unfriend me and block me. I would get major spiritual attacks when I would post the things I was posting. FB is a spiritual portal. I remember at 5:00 a.m. one morning I was awakened by this horrible feeling and I knew that someone had entered my FB page and indeed, I was right. At the very moment that I had felt the most horrible feeling in my physical body, I saw that a strong Satanist had entered my FB. And yes, I would friend request some Satanists, I was trying to show Jesus to everyone, but when I saw the level of attack upon my physical body that it was taking, I had to slow it down. It would knock me out and force me to lay down on my bed for a long time with no strength at all. I was really drained. It was not normal at all. I was forced to fast for days to be able to counterattack the attacks that were coming toward me.

Meanwhile, my son began to become too anxious to focus on his school and no matter how hard I tried to have him do well in his classes, we were both too overwhelmed with stress to continue trying. He just could not focus. I also had no money and even though we were staying in a Motel paid by the government, I still had to come up with food. I didn't have money for that. I had no choice but to start pan handling. It was by far the most painful and humiliating thing I ever had to do for money. I also left my son alone in the room and went to the street across the Motel and pan handled for a couple of hours. I would cry my heart out as I stood there with my cardboard and saw person after person just pass by me, stare at me and give me nothing. Occasionally some person would give me some money. But the truth is most of them ignored me and gave me weird looks and I only made $20 bucks at the most. I remember thinking: "So this is what the real poor people feel like on an everyday routine!" They feel like scum and totally worthless.

As I stood under the hot sun, holding up my sign and being utterly humiliated, I knew that God wanted me to experience that moment, not because He hates me, but because He loves the poor people, He loves all those single moms that are going through the same things, and He wants me to be their voice in this world. I have always known that He wants me to write all these things down and show the world just how unrighteous, how selfish and greedy they are. Thus, knowing that gave me strength to endure the pain. I felt like fainting at times, but I would tell myself that I was just an actress in a movie playing a role. I would tell myself that I am the daughter of the King of kings of this entire universe and that being the daughter of a King made me a princess. I would tell myself that as a daughter of a King I was rich and beautiful and smart and like a celebrity and that what was happening to me was just as if I was working in a movie as an actress and that all this nightmare would soon fade away.

My son got to see just how selfish people are and he was deeply wounded by this, but I also knew that God wanted him to experience this so that he may be wise about the world we live in and I know in my heart that someday all those experiences will turn out for good and that God will use that to bring out something great from it.

There were some scary nights for us in that Motel. One night we had not eaten all day and I was really scared that we may not get food again the next day. My son and I went to sleep so hungry. I don't think I had ever been that hungry and scared about the hunger I had in my entire life. The next day we got to eat. But now my son and I truly know what hungry, poor people are experiencing and it is no joke. Now I can understand why the crime rate among the poor communities is so high. I am not justifying stealing, but I can understand how they can become that desperate. It really is a scary thing to go hungry.

Throughout all these experiences, I was still posting warnings in FB and no one in it had a clue of what I was going through. My brother happened to live near the area where we were, and he was sent to us like an angel. Even though I barely see him or talk to him, he came to our rescue during this season. He brought me things to cook with and utensils to eat with and because of that I was able to buy groceries instead of eating out and I saved money. This saved me. I am so grateful for my brother. I honestly don't know what I would have done without the things he lent us. He also brought us food from time to time from the restaurant that he worked at. There was a shopping center across the motel and a basketball court, and I would walk there with my son and we would spend our time there. He got to play a lot of basketball and even made some friends in the court. I would worship God by a soccer field near the court while he would play basketball. This was how I would spend the time with him.

After four months of living there, they finally found a spot for us in a shelter and they sent a bus to pick us up and transport us to the shelter. We got there late at night and I must say, it was the worst night for me. The place reminded me of when I had been in the mental hospital. The rooms and the beds were just simply awful. Then in the morning they told me that for me to stay there, I had to get vaccinated. I said, hell no! I had been researching and posting in FB about how vaccines are harmful to our health, about how they have confirmed that vaccines cause autism and a bunch of other health issues, about how there is an agenda to depopulate the world through vaccines, and I was posting and warning that they were going to implant the RFID chip which is the mark of the beast, without permission, through vaccines or when they withdraw blood to donate it to the red cross.

And he causeth all, both small and great, rich and poor, free and bond, to receive a mark in their right hand, or in their foreheads: And that no man might buy or sell, save he that had the mark, or the name of the beast, or the number of his name. Revelation 13: 16-17

I told them that I would go to another shelter. They told me that every shelter would require that I get vaccinated. Thus, I called my sister and asked her if she would let me live with her. She said no. I knew that asking my brother to live with him was useless as well. He would most certainly say no to me even more than my sister. Thus, I told my son: "We are leaving this place immediately! Grab your things and let's go!" He freaked out and said that why don't I just get vaccinated? He knew we had nowhere to go. I told him under no circumstances will I take any vaccines or let them vaccinate you! My son became angry with me and started fighting me and tried to convince me to take the vaccine because we had nowhere to go. I told him to have faith in God. I told him that I knew somehow God will provide for us to sleep somewhere during the night. But that we are not taking any vaccines. He was still mad at me and fighting me, but he had no choice but to obey me. We left walking with our bags and went to eat at a McDonalds. There I decided to finally come out in FB explaining my situation to everyone and see if someone would help me. I had over one thousand people in my timeline. Only a handful of people offered help. They offered me to go to their place, but they were out of the state. I had nowhere to go and FB was not going to be of any help. I prayed and asked God what should I do? He instructed me to check my child support card. But I found that to be strange because I knew that the child support money was not to be there just yet. However, I checked and to my surprise there was money in it. My son's father had sent me his child support early that month which was a very rare event.

I took a bus with my son to a hotel and we stayed there for the night. I remember when I slept in that hotel's bed, I felt so good. I had not slept in a good bed for a very long time!

Suddenly, a friend of mine wrote to me in FB and offered me to go to stay at her place. I was so relived. This was one of the girls that I took in my first apartment and helped out for a couple of months. I asked Richard if he can give me a ride to her house from the hotel and he said yes. This was on New Year's Eve. He came to get me with his friends and when he drove me to her house, my friend was nowhere to be found. Then she called and told me that she changed her mind about me staying with her and then sent me to go to her other friend's house, saying that she would help me. I could not believe this! I wanted for the ground to open up and swallow me. I was so embarrassed! We then drove to the other friend's house, who was also my friend; and of course, she had no idea what was going on, she was in the middle of hosting a New Year's Eve party at her home with her family and there was no space for us in there. I was more embarrassed by now and I didn't have a clue as to what I was supposed to do now.

Richard and his friends collected money and paid for us to sleep in a motel. This place was very sinful, and I spent the entire night in that room battling demons that were attacking me throughout the whole night. I was physically shaking the whole night from the attacks; something that has never happened to me before. The next day, another friend of mine whom I have not seen since we graduated from high school, almost twenty years ago, offered to give me money. He came over and paid $50 for me to stay in there one more night. We still needed to get more help, I had no car, no money, no nothing. My son and I would spend the day in the library that was close to the motel and Richard was the one trying to help me find somewhere to go.

What a horrible situation I was in. Yet I never stopped posting in FB the warnings of the things to come. My posting on FB became my escape because they gave me a sense of purpose and I hate wasting time. I hate feeling unproductive. I also was upset with the world at the level of greed, selfishness and wickedness that I was experiencing firsthand and I was letting everyone in FB know how filthy and wicked people really are! I also kept on writing to my online mystery cyber boyfriend. I was telling him everything that I was experiencing. That also was my escape and those two things kept me going. My son would also escape on his phone. Playing games and talking through social media. And as much as I would have preferred for him to be playing sports, riding bikes, learning an instrument, instead of being in social media, I had no choice but to let him. We had nothing else that we could do. We were trapped!

Moreover, I was out of time and out of money concerning the motel I had stayed in for three days now. We were now in the library with all our belongings and just waiting to see if Richard can find a place for us to go. The library was closing, and my son and I were in the streets now, waiting to see where we would sleep that night. We were walking around the streets at night, near the library, but everything was closed and dark and scary. After a long time of waiting for Richard, very late in the night, like at 2:00 a.m., he finally found a homeless ministry that was willing to take us. Thankfully, even though they came over to us very late, we didn't have to spend the whole night alone and in the streets. As I remember all this, I marvel at just how much Richard sacrificed his time, money and energy to help me. The man really has a heart of gold!

CHAPTER 16

HOMELESS MINISTRY
IN MIAMI, FL

We spent the night at the Pastor's home. She was a grieving mother, whom had just lost her teenage only son in a terrible accident. Her son had been playing basketball with some friends and their ball had fallen into a place next to the court, where there was high voltage electricity boxes and he went in there to get the ball and was electrocuted to death. My son and I slept in her young boy's room which still had all his things in there. This accident had just happened. The sadness I felt concerning this was unreal. The thought of that happening to me is unbearable. Also, I was extremely uncomfortable sleeping in a bed of someone whom had just passed away. But there was nothing I can do about it.

The next morning, we had breakfast with the woman Pastor and the Pastor of this homeless ministry. They were not a couple. They were just working together in this ministry. She was married with someone else who also lived in the home where we were staying. But he was not too into the church or the ministry. He also was in a deep depression because of his son's death and seemed to have a bit of a grudge against the ministry his wife was so devoted to. After breakfast, we drove around the Miami area with two other homeless people. These two were a homeless couple that they were also helping. We drove to different places to pick up food that was being donated to them and then we went to their warehouse where we all helped them unpack the truck and organize the warehouse. The homeless man that they were helping was very ill. He had a fever. Yet we went with them to help a woman that belonged to their church, to move. She was a rich lady with fancy, marble furniture and we all moved out this furniture and helped them move her. We all spent the whole day moving her, we all were sweating, my son even got a sharp pain in his pelvic area from lifting heavy things. We were all exhausted by the end of the day.

The owner of the house we moved paid the Pastor for this job, however, none of us got paid for working. We got to eat "for free" and we were thanked by them, but it was not paid, even though we all worked extremely hard and I know that what we did is a job that deserves a great pay check to be given to. But they were sheltering my son and me, so I was not complaining, and I was actually very glad to help. However, after all that hard labor, the homeless young man, who was the one who lifted most of the heaviest things, became even more sick by now. I felt sorry for him. Yet they ended up dropping him off under a bridge. He asked to be taken to the hospital, but they didn't do that. They dropped him off under a bridge. This broke my heart and I think they noticed, thus they told me that they had been helping him for a while, but that he was a drug addict and that he was greatly irresponsible. His girlfriend supposedly was just as bad as he was and they just could not help them anymore, thus they dropped him off under a bridge in Downtown even though he had a really high fever, and supposedly he claimed that his stool had blood in it.

I was still horrified by all this! I thought that if they could not help him anymore with anything else, at the least, they should not have made him carry the marble furniture all day long the way they did. He worked the hardest out of all of us, and he was the most ill!

The pain in my heart only increased day by day. When we finished that hard day of work, I was satisfied with the way my son and I helped them and thought that helping them that way was a great opportunity for me to thank them for helping me. But to my horrific surprise, when we got to the home of the woman whom I was staying with, the male Pastor sits on the sofa, looks at me in my eyes and tells me: "I just want you to know that you are not helping us, but we are the ones helping you"… Oh how that hurt me! This is what everyone does to me! They make me do major physical labors for them, that if I would not do them, they would most certainly need to pay someone else to get it done, and then they want to pretend that I am not helping them at all and that they are the only ones helping me instead. Why??? Why do they always fall for this temptation of exploiting the poor and the needy and then pretending that they are the only ones helping them? I will tell you why they do this, because they can! Because they can do this and get away with it over and over again! That is why they do it!

After I heard this man say this me, I swallowed hard and held back my tears and just nodded my head as if I agreed to this. Next, as if I was not tired and sad enough and as if things could not get any worse, my son got sick. I think he picked it up from the homeless man that was coughing up a storm in the same car we were in. Now I am freaking out, because every time my son gets a fever, I just have the most panicky feeling in the world creep up within me. Since throughout his childhood he got several feveral seizures that scared me to death! The crazy thing about all this is that during the night, before my son got sick, I had a dream where a woman whom I had known from the apostate churches, came up to me and warned me that if I didn't stop posting the things that I was posting in FB, she was going to take my son away from me for good. In the dream, I begged her to please don't do that and she insisted that she was going to do it because the things I was posting were making her look bad.

That morning after I had this dream, my son woke up sick. Also, the lady I lived with was a prophetess and would receive many prophetic visions as well. She woke up and shared with me a dream that the Lord gave her. She told me that she had a dream that she saw my cousin Andrew, the crazy uncle that had been in jail for doing bad things to his wife and step children. She said she saw him with candles lit and that he was doing witchcraft against me. She said in the dream, she told him not to do that, that those things were evil and not from God, but that he said to her that he felt very afraid about me and that he had to do it.

Moreover, during the evening, my son's cold was getting bad, so I needed to get him ginger root from the food market, because I always give him ginger tea and it helps to cure him faster. But I didn't have a car and neither did the woman that I was staying with. Her husband also didn't have a car. I didn't know how to resolve this. All my options would make me a bad mom. I could not make my son to walk with me because he was too sick. I could not leave him alone with her husband because I really didn't know him. The only option I saw most fit was to leave him in the library which was still right across the house we were staying. I only had left him alone once in the motel for a couple of hours, it was always a horrific thing for me to do. But I had no choice. I decided to leave him in the library by himself while I walked with the lady to get him ginger and I told him that if they closed the library to walk to the house and meet me there. The house was literally across. All it took was two minutes. However, it was a dangerous road to cross because it had a lot of traffic. But I had to lower his fever and I needed things from the market to get that done. Thus, when I was in the market buying the things, the husband of this lady called, and I hear the words: "Your son was run over by a car"! My heart sunk and I became numb. We walked back to the house immediately and there was my son bleeding from his head.

The ambulance came and we left to the hospital. They performed a brain scan and they had to put fifteen stitches on his head because of how deep the wound was on the top of his head. They instructed us to not let him go to school for ten days, or not to let him read or even watch TV. He was to be resting the whole time and just not do anything with his mind. He also still had a cold and I still had to tackle the fever. I didn't sleep all night long, lowering his fever, praying and weeping over him. He began to hallucinate and say weird things, I think it might have to do with the Tylenol and the Motrin, he had done that before. It always has scared me to death. I could not stop thinking about the dream I had the night before and about the dream the lady I was staying with had with my cousin. Could any of this be a result of witchcraft? I prayed in tongues and prayed and prayed. I also wondered if there was a spirit of death in the room we were staying, since her young boy had just recently passed away as well. Later, I found out that indeed, there was a strong spirit of death in that room, because I found all the violent, satanic video games that young boy used to play in that room. I told the lady about them and asked her how in the world would she allow these games here, when she was a teacher of the word of God? I warned her that those games were super demonic and bring a lot of demons of death and destruction upon everyone in the house. She told me they used to buy them for her son and the father would even spend hours playing them with him. I told her to throw them away and she did!

But I was truly horrified by this, this is the reason why I can't take part in churches now a days. I don't understand how Christians can devote so much time and energy to working in secular jobs and then serving in church and just hand over their children to Satan as their babysitter? This is something I see over and over in every church I have been to. The adults always too busy working and serving while the devil is feasting on their children.

Furthermore, while I am trying to restore my son back to health, I then come across a new challenge that completely blew me away! The Pastor wanted me and my son to hop on his van all day long as we had been doing and continue to work with him in all the errands that he has to do through the day. Which was always a lot of hard labor. I told him that my son could not be going anywhere and that I needed to stay there right next to him, feeding him and taking care of him. To my surprise, he got upset with me and extremely offended that I refused to go with him. He began to get a grudge against me and started to tell the lady I was staying with that I was lazy and didn't want to work and that she needed to take me out of her home. He claimed that my son's injury was no big deal and that he was fine. I could not believe he said I was lazy, when by then I had helped him move out a woman from her home, I had gone with them all over Miami and helped them gather food and work in their warehouse organizing the food. I had woken up early to prepare food for the homeless and go to the beach to feed the homeless and pray for them. I had worked hard just serving them and cleaning the place I was staying in, I even spring cleaned the fridge and would wash by hand all the dirty pots that were being used to cook the meals for the homeless. He still had the audacity to claim that I was lazy!

Thankfully, the lady fought with him because when I first moved in, she heard the Lord tell her, that I was His work. She said to me that she received His confirmation to take me in and to help me. She also had a dream shortly after my arrival in her home, where she saw two beautiful angels holding big presents in their hands, they walked toward me and handed over to me those big gifts and then she was told that I was to be rewarded for the work I was sent to do there in her home and that they wanted for her to learn from me how to pray.

I was very relieved to hear all that and she told me not to worry about the Pastor and his temper tantrum, because she also knew that there was something wrong with him. She said God had been showing her that he was inclining toward the flesh and that he was not pleasing God. She also said that she knew he was a very controlling man and if anyone ever resisted him, he would get like that. She told me to ignore him because she was the one helping me, and I was in her home and to feel at home. We would then pray together early in the morning hours and share with each other what the Lord would show us. I would clean the house as much as possible for her, but I noticed that she was having a hard time with the chores that I should do. One moment she would want me to clean the house and the next moment she would want me to not clean the house and "feel at home" and relax and take it easy because she wanted to help me. Even my son noticed her conflict about this, and I just didn't know what to do or think.

Valentine's Day was coming, and this was a very important day for her. She was an illegal immigrant and the way she would earn a living was creating gift boxes for holidays and selling them in the streets. I went with her to buy all the things that she gets to prepare the gift boxes and I was a bit hesitant in helping her build all these gifts boxes, because the Lord had been showing me the truth about all these pagan holidays and their demonic origins. Those were also the type of revelations that I was showing everyone in FB. So I felt guilty of sin if I was to work on doing those Valentines gifts. But I heard the Spirit of God say to me to help her anyway. He then said, I want you to help her and see what happens after that. Then He reminded me of the show that I used to watch on TV called *Wife Swap*. This is a show that psychologists created to put people who are totally opposite to each other together and have them live together for two weeks. One week they must submit to their opposite's rules and the other week they switch. They end up learning much from each other. Thus, one time the Lord told me to look at my life as a huge "Wife Swap" episode.

I remembered that, and I decided to help her make this gift boxes. I spend hours and hours wrapping them up and constructing them. I made like forty boxes one night and was exhausted, that was like three or four hours of manual labor. Meanwhile my son would just sit there watching us work and watching TV. While we worked together on these things, I noticed that she would spend a lot of time on the phone talking to the Pastor and then her demeanor changed. She then snapped at me and claimed that I don't do anything and that I only did like three boxes. I cried so hard after I heard that. The pain was unbearable by now. My son came up to me and began to cheer me up and say to me to ignore her and that obviously that was not true. Her husband was there and saw me in tears as well and he consoled me as well and told me to ignore her, and that she does that same thing to him all the time. He claimed that he would give her $100 and that she would say he only gave her $10. Still nothing they would say to me would console me. I could not take this abuse anymore. I had passed by too many people pulling this stunt on me over and over again. I felt exhausted! I just wanted for my labor to be counted as something. I wanted to feel appreciated for once.

Her husband shared with me that she had not been a good mother to her son or a good wife because she would always put the homeless ministry before them. He said her son fought with her a lot and used to tell her that she loved her ministry more than him. He said that was the reason he was not part of the ministry. She would take better care of the homeless than of them. This is the main problem in most Christian homes. They are light in the streets, but darkness at home.

I will never forget my beautiful little son, standing on front of me while I was crying a river because of what she had said to me after I had worked so hard all night long, and he looked at me in the eye as if he was a grown man and told me that I was the best mother in the world! He said that I was an amazing woman and hardworking and loving and to not let any of these people knock me down. I honestly think He was possessed by the Holy Spirit because the anointing I felt coming upon me as he spoke to me was incredible!

After that speech, I did feel better and very proud of my son and I was able to see that God was indeed working greatly in him. Later, we were in the library and I ran into a woman whom claimed to have witnessed the car accident my son had crossing the street. She told me that she knows that it was a miracle that he didn't die. She said that she saw as if angels carried him toward the sidewalk and sort of blocked his fall. The car that hit him was going pretty fast and the driver kept on going and was never found.

However, all these painful things were piling up and piling up and one day, my son had enough and lost it! We were alone in the house and he threw himself on the floor of the room we were staying in and he cried really hard and really loud and began asking God why do we have to be so poor? Why can't he give us money to get our own place? Why do we need to suffer this much? And he was angry, and I can see the anger just pouring out of his heart through his mouth and fists. He was kicking the floor and looked as if he wanted to punch something.

Keep in mind he was still wounded from the car accident and all these things were happening during the days he was supposed to be resting. Luckily for us, there was a punching doll in the back patio from where we stayed, and he started to punch that thing and it would make him feel better. That became his therapy in that place. He loved punching that thing! Unfortunately, it was not ours, it was the neighbors and eventually they had to tell him to stop.

In addition, the lady I was staying with became unpredictable! One moment she was my best friend and the next moment she was the Pastor's best friend instead, and that man wanted me to be kicked out of there badly. I don't know what it is about me, but people love to hate me. Even if they don't know me at all. This guy got a huge grudge against me and he was working very hard to transfer it to the lady whom I was living with. I think it had a lot to do with FB. He saw the things I was posting, and it was exposing the prosperity gospel preachers as wolves dressed in sheep and he belonged to those churches. Thus, I think this was the reason he thought I was the devil. I wanted to quit FB and I would tell God that how can he have me posting these things in FB and at the same time have me living with these kinds of Christians, but the Lord insisted that I continue FB and endure their wrath.

"When thou art come unto the land which the Lord thy God giveth thee, and shalt possess it, and shalt dwell therein, and shalt say, I will set a king over me, like as all the nations that are about me; Thou shalt in any wise set him king over thee, whom the Lord thy God shall choose: one from among thy brethren shalt thou set king over thee: thou mayest not set a stranger over thee, which is thy brother. But he shall not multiply horses to himself, nor cause the people to return to Egypt, to the end that he should multiply horses: for as much as the Lord hath said unto you, Ye shall henceforth return no more that way. Neither shall he multiply wives to himself, that his heart turn not away: neither shall he greatly multiply to himself silver and gold."Deuteronomy 17:14-17

If there arise among you a prophet, or a dreamer of dreams, and giveth thee a sign or a wonder, And a sign or the wonder come to pass, whereof he spake unto thee, saying, Let us go after other gods which thou hast not known, and let us serve them; Thou shalt not hearken unto the words of that prophet, or that dreamer of dreams: for the Lord your God proveth you, to know

**whether ye love the Lord your God
with all your heart and with all your
soul. Ye shall walk after the Lord your
God, and fear Him, and keep His commandments, and obey His voice, and ye
shall serve Him, and cleave unto Him.
Deuteronomy 13:1-4**

The prosperity gospel is a false teaching and these two verses in the Bible, among many others, expose that. These false prosperity gospel preachers are wolves in sheep's clothing. Not only are they robbing the people their money, they are the ones at fault for the disaster we now see in our society. They are the ones at fault for these single parents having to choose between abandoning their underage children to go to work or to become homeless for not having the courage to abandon their young children. They are the ones responsible for the church surrendering to the evil and corrupt government the care of the poor and the needy. That was never the government's responsibility, that was and still is the responsibility of the church. Which was the reason why the church was not supposed to pay any taxes. These people are frauds and they are also misleading the masses to worship other gods just as we were warned here in the book of Deuteronomy. They not only, **not teach** the people to celebrate the real biblical feasts that Jesus Christ/ Yeshua Hamashiac, instructed us to observe, they actually go as far as to teach people to celebrate the pagan feasts that our Lord abominates.

All the holidays that we celebrate here in America are from pagan origin and a blatant offense and mockery to our Lord. Starting with Christmas, a day that many of our Lord's enemies were actually born in and a day were most definitely our Savior was not born in. This entire feast is of a very dark, satanic and perverted origin and it was so bad that in the early years of the creation of our Nation, this holiday was banned from America. You can do your research online and see that what I am saying here is the truth. Research the true meaning of Christmas and all the true symbolic meanings of the trees, Santa/Satan Clause, etc...In the same manner, everything else we celebrate here in our churches of America is pagan and of a very dark origin. St. Valentines, Halloween, Easter, Sunday mass/ worship, etc...We have been deceived by these false preachers and the time has come to wake up from your slumber church! Learn the truth about the origins of all these holidays and find out for yourselves that our "favorite preachers" are the ones the Bible warns us to not follow. You have been warned!

One day the lady Pastor sat me down in her kitchen and began telling me a real-life experience that she had. She said that there was once this undercover cop that was pretending to be a homeless man sleeping in the street corner by where she slept, because she was homeless too. She said she could not believe how this man was able to endure months and months of living the way he was living. She said every day he would be in the same spot and was all dirty looking and everyone thought he was a real homeless man. But he was a cop who had been assigned to do that so that they can catch a bunch of drug lords that were selling drugs near the area. She said the cop would tell her that one day he was going to tell her to run away and to go far.

He would tell her that when that day came and he would tell her that, that she needed to heed his warning and just go. That day came and she obeyed his warning and took off and they busted hundreds of drug dealers. She couldn't believe that for months this cop lived like a real homeless person to bust all those people. She didn't know when she was telling me this story about her life that God was speaking to me. I then saw that I was like that cop and that the reason I was going through all this nightmare was to bust all the wicked people in His body who are pretending to be righteous and holy.

Meanwhile, the Pastor began threatening me concerning my son and that I had to put him in school and that if I didn't put him in school, that he was going to report me to the authorities. But the man had forgotten that I had a letter from the hospital stating that my son was supposed to be out of school for two weeks to rest from his head injury. Still that didn't seem to matter, he was enraged! From time to time he would get the lady to turn against me too. She decided to bring to the house a woman from my last apostate, mega church that I used to be in. She wanted the woman to minister to me and to put me in my place because by now she was taking the side of the Pastor.

When this woman came over, I was deeply humiliated by her. She stood on front of me and placed her hand on my head so as to prophesy to me, but I stopped her because I no longer let anyone place their hands on my head. She became deeply offended by my resistance and began to say that I was lost and with no guidance. That I was a bad mother for not having a job and that I was making my son suffer for not being more diligent. I ran inside the room where I stayed and bowed myself down and began to weep to the Lord and prayed for Him to have mercy on me. I cried and cried and the Christian woman whom thought of herself as someone very important, she came looking for me to continue to rebuke me and when she saw that I was on my knees crying, she paused for a moment and then left. There was a group in the house of about seven people from the church and they were all gossiping about me as if I was this crazy person who was rebellious and lazy and not fit to have custody of my son. That day I felt smaller than scum! The pride in all these people was tangible and they sure know how to make someone feel inferior!

But this behavior in people toward me was becoming a pattern. Everywhere I went, everyone seemed to behave the same way with me. They all looked down on me and exploited me and thought of me as a lazy leach who deserved to be exploited because I didn't want to work.

And while they exploited me to their delight without any mercy, they would have the audacity of criticizing me for not being with my son and attending him as if I was not busy working for them, and as if I had nothing to do but to be with my son and attend him. There was a no-win situation for me. If I attended my son and cared for him, I was a terrible mother for not working and providing for him, but if I was busy working, whether in the tasks they made me do for them or in jobs, I was a terrible mother for neglecting him. Who made these rules? How can this scenario be just or fair in any way? There are no good options for me here! My heart was broken in a million pieces and the only ones whom seemed to understand me were God, my son and this lady's husband. The lady would fight with the

Pastor and tell him that he was mistaken at one moment and then she was kicking me out the next moment. This was insane! I started to have to think once again, where in the world will I live next?

Finally, the Pastor convinced the lady to kick me out and she did! I ended up calling Richard, and my beloved Richard came to my rescue once again. I really didn't want to involve Richard this much in my situation because at the moment I still believed that he wasn't the husband that God had for me. I still believed that God was going to eventually bring me the online mystery boyfriend I had been writing to all that time. But I had nowhere else to go. I really had no one else to call. Everyone had turned their backs on me. Both my siblings and only family would not let me live with them, my parents both are passed away and the shelter was a nightmare and a vaccination scam!

I didn't even know Richard would take me either, because the last time he had told me he could not take me because he lived with his mother and it was a very small place. But somehow, when I called him and explained to him everything that was happening, he had the heart to open his home to me and my son and thus he came to pick us up at the woman's house. The lady was very surprise that he came to get us, because she had been saying to me that if I wasn't in sin, then God would provide a place for me to go to, but because I was outside of the will of God, that was the reason I was without any place to go. Thus, she kicked me out of her home, knowing I had no place to go to and when she saw that Richard picked me up, she freaked out!

She knew who Richard is, he was the one who connected me to them in the first place. He had also visited their church with me there and someone had chosen him to prophesy over his life and the prophesy he got was incredible, about prosperity and business, and I remember she mentioned to me about how great that prophesy to him was!

I remember that right before I knew where I was going next, I heard the Spirit of God say to me that once again He would deliver me from my enemies. Thus, He did! Richard came and drove us to his home.

CHAPTER 17

RICHARD'S HOME

Right after I moved out of this lady's house, I found out that the Pastor had contacted my cousins and that they told him that indeed, I was crazy and that I was lazy and that I didn't want to work. Thus, the Pastor called my son's father and began saying that I needed psychiatric medication and that he needed to take my son away from me because I was not fit to be a mother and that I was seriously mentally ill, the only thing with this was that the Pastor whom thought of himself as someone very wise had not really called my son's father. He actually called Richard's phone number thinking it was my son's father's phone number and Richard had played along and pretended to be my son's father and went along with everything this man said about me. Not only did he trick the Pastor, he recorded everything he said. I was blown away by this! God is awesome! The Pastor never noticed he spoke to the wrong person!

I was completely wounded thou, had this Pastor truly reached my son's father, he would have destroyed me with his lies! But the Lord didn't allow him to destroy me. My son's father already was confused about me because of the lies my cousins told him, had he heard this same lies from a Christian Pastor, chances are that he would have been convinced of these lies. But Richard was very wise and saved me one more time. However, even thou that Pastor was not able to deceive my ex, my son's father still took me once again to court. When I went to court, I stood on front of a judge who blatantly insulted me, humiliated me on front of everyone to the point of making me wish for the ground to open-up and swallow me in. He called me a bad mother and a failure of a mother. He had no intentions of finding out the reason my financial situation had gotten so bad as to making me homeless was that I had been pinned between the wall and the sword and that I was forced to choose between going to a job and abandoning several underage children and putting them in danger or to stay put and keep watching over them.

All the judge cared to hear was that I had not been able to provide for my son and because of that my son was better off with his father. This time was different than all the other times, this time the judge actually wanted to give my son to his father, and to my surprise, his father was moved to compassion and told the judge that he would give me another chance to get my life in order. The judge seemed puzzled by his response and gave him a stare as if disapproving of this decision, but he had no choice but to let me keep my son and then he requested for us to be evaluated by a psychiatrist and he would then make a decision concerning the custody of my son.

Thankfully, the entire court case was successfully closed, after the psychiatrist sent out his documents about me. The psychiatrist was the best of them all according to his credentials and he told my son's father that I was the best wife any man in this world could have and that I was an excellent mother. He also said that women like me are rare to find these days! My son's father was stunned and that was the end of our court days.

Furthermore, Richard and I called the best friend of the female Pastor I stayed with when I was homeless. She knew me and even prayed with me during my time with them and we told her to tell the Pastor and the lady to stop lying about me and to know that God was looking out for me because he provided me a new place and he also didn't allow the Pastor to notice that he called the wrong person. She couldn't believe how all of this played out, but she certainly testified that she knew they had been wrong about me.

Unfortunately, these people are the only ones in the Miami area with a homeless ministry. It marvels me that I used to go the biggest Hispanic church in the United States of America, where the temple cost millions of dollars to build and the Pastors of that church live in a million-dollar home, yet they don't have a homeless ministry. They just send out family food boxes once a week. That is all the help they provide in this type of department and that is not even good enough for any homeless person, because these types of foods are to be cooked and they have no homes to cook them in. Thus, the only Christian homeless ministry in Miami, outside of the government is the one I was in and to my rude awakening they exploit those whom they claim to be helping and they truly don't know how to rehabilitate any drug or alcohol addicts. Also, they don't know how to truly help a single mother "be a good mother" and they really don't know how to get a wounded, old and traumatized veteran out of the streets. They only know how to put everyone to work, as if everyone was a twenty-five-year-old healthy male, and they only know how to keep them in poverty because they keep them way too busy every day working for free!

I want my readers to know that this is how the devil gets to frame innocent, hardworking people and this is how he gets everyone in their life to cast them aside and keep them oppressed and looking as if they deserve their calamities. Is easy for Satan to frame good people, when we live in a world where the design of God for the family and for society has been totally twisted and when the whole world expects everyone to work in a secular job and maintain themselves, without thinking about the fact that not everyone has someone sound minded and good hearted to leave their children with while they go out to work and not everyone is physically or mentally able to work in formal jobs like everyone else.

> **If any man or woman that believeth have widows, let them relieve them, and let not the church be charged; that it may relieve them that are widows indeed. 1 Timothy 5:16**

This verse shows that the family members of any widows were responsible to look out for these women, so that the church would not have to have that burden upon them and like that they can afford to help those widows without any family members to help them. Here we see that no where was the government involved in helping these people. We also see they were not expecting them to go to work, they were to be sustained by them. If these widows had children, which many of them did, they already had a full time job. Those days, day cares and public school's were non existent. Mothers were not just homemakers, they were home schooling their children as well in the knowledge and love of God. An extremely important, full time job and what is missing in our society today and the results of it are evident.

For ye have the poor always with you; but Me ye have not always. Matthew 26:11

For the poor shall never cease out of the land: therefore I command thee, saying, thou shalt open thine hand wide unto thy brother, to thy poor, and to thy needy, in thy land. Deuteronomy 15:11

After much pondering about this ministry I realized that only the rich people can truly help the homeless, the drug addicts, the elderly and the mentally disable. It takes money to place them in a decent place where they can have someone help them rehabilitate. A place where instead of having them work like slaves, they can focus on getting closer to God, reading His word, fasting, praying, exercising their bodies and just getting healthier. This ministry that I was in for a short period of time is led by poor people trying to help really poor people. It just isn't good enough. They don't have the provision needed to really make a difference. They may be feeding the homeless and giving them a relief from time to time, but they can't rehabilitate them. They just don't have the money to do that. I noticed the leaders of the ministry were all struggling financially themselves and the entire ministry depends on charity from others. I noticed that a lot of the food they were giving to the homeless and the poor had been expired even for over a year. I thought that was unacceptable! I noticed that the lady who took me in was being majorly exploited and even mistreated by this Pastor who was in charge of the whole ministry. I also thought that was unacceptable! This lady would acknowledge to me that she knew he would mistreat her, yet she was enduring it.

It is truly a shame to see so many mega churches in so many cities in the US, yet so many homeless people in all these cities. That is a sign of the times we are living in. The love of many has surely grown cold. And many of these mega churches feel good about themselves because they donate lots of money to many other poor countries and help the poor in many other places, but they fail to realize that as a Church, they are called to help the poor in their own neighborhood first. They fail to realize that God never intended for the poor to be helped by their government. The Church was the one appointed by God to take care of its own! But the church has conveniently passed down that responsibility to the government and as a result we are about to enter hard core communism and socialism that oppress the people and makes everyone poor.

I mentioned that rich people are the ones who can truly help all these types of people, but I intentionally left out one specific group of people. Single mothers! Single mothers cannot be helped even by rich people in general, because the design of God was never for them to leave their babies to go out to work. Thus, as long as women keep handing over their children to be indoctrinated by Hollywood, the evil government whom is in control of the public-school system and the media, our society will only continue to spiral out of control and the love of many will only continue to grow cold! Children were never meant to be apart from their mothers throughout their childhood. Mothers are the ones whom keep them feeling loved and protected and affirmed and as long as we take that away from the youth, we will continue to see a youth with a dark, hardened heart and rebellious to all authority!

Moreover, coming to live with Richard was not easy. He really had no space for us. He lived in a two-bedroom trailer with his mother and with a friend of his who was also homeless. His friend slept in the sofa. The only place where my son and I were able to sleep was on the floor next to Richard's bed. I would put a matt which was the sofa, every night on the floor and slept there with my son for months. I put my son in school and walked him there every morning and picked him up every afternoon. It was not so close, but there was no school bus that would come to our area. Because we live in a trailer Park that is for Seniors and not for children. This was supposed to be for his mother and Richard was supposed to be here temporarily.

Things in Richard's home were a bit crazy, because his mom didn't really want his homeless friend to continue to live there and then she also began feeling upset at me because I didn't have a formal job. Once again, I was in the same predicament I always found myself in. God is ordaining me to stay home with my son and take good care of him and the house and to seek Him during my time in the home and at the same time I was been tortured by Richard's mom to get a job. In the other hand, Richard's homeless friend who was staying with us, was a bit jealous of our relationship and began to cause division between Richard and me.

Richard didn't really pressure me to get a job. He tried his best to help me. But his friend's words against me and his own mother's words against me would cause him to change with me as well. His mother would also involve the neighbors in our situation and other people outside the home and they too would influence Richard's thinking about me. There was just too many fights breaking out between all of us and it became unbearable to me.

I was under a great amount of stress and even though I was tempted to get a job, I just could not leave my son alone in the house because I didn't trust Richard's friend with my son and I also thought the fights between his mother and the guy were too intense to have my son alone in there with them. I also didn't want my son to walk to school and back all by himself. He was too young, and this was not the best of neighborhood either. I had to walk him, there was no negotiating this! I was also having to walk on egg shells during these days, because we were in the middle of a psychological evaluation, where my son, his father and I had to go once a week to see the psychiatrist that had been assigned to us from court. Thus, God was right in commanding me to not leave my son alone and to take good care of him, because they could have easily taken him away from me, if I had gotten a job and something happened with him while I was working. Richard was out working all day long, and sometimes his friend worked with Richard, but most of the time he stayed home, which is why his mom was so upset at him.

To make a long story short, after six months of surviving the fights, I moved out! I could not take the stress anymore, and I asked God if I can move away and He said that even though that was not really His perfect will, He gave me permission to leave because of the circumstances. This answer to my prayer came to me through my son. By this time, my son was very skilled in hearing the voice of God. I also asked my son to pray and seek God concerning where we should go, because I had no idea where to go and he mentioned one name to me. I was stunned to hear that name because my son had no idea that I had talked to this woman when I moved in with Richard and told her what happened to me, and she told me that if I needed a place to live, I can always stay at her mother's house who lived in Miami. I had completely forgotten about that conversation and about that option.

My son was hearing the voice of God better than me by then, because I was so overwhelmed with stress and tension that the voice of the Lord began to shut off. After my son mentioned her name, I called her and then my neighbor drove us and all our belongings to my friend's mother's home.

My sheep hear my voice, and I know them, and they follow Me. John 10:27

CHAPTER 18

My Friend's Mother's Home

When I arrived here, I was physically, emotionally and spiritually drained. My face had a horrific acne outbreak. It was almost just as bad as the outbreak I experienced when I gave birth to my son. My face was unrecognizable! I looked as if I had the chicken pox. It made this whole ordeal that much more embarrassing to me. I didn't have a job, or a phone, or a car, or any money. I was deeply saddened that I was still going through all of this and extremely ashamed of my situation. My friend's mom was very nice and help-ful, but I can tell she also was stunned and horrified at my situation. I was able to hear her talking on the phone to her friends about how terrible my situation was and that she could not believe that I didn't even have a phone. I was in great emotional pain. My ego was also smashed to the max. I put my son in school and here I was able to get him a private bus to come and get him. His father helped me to pay for it. As the days went by, I started to feel the tension between my friend's mother concerning my getting a job. In this house, even though I still didn't approve of leaving my underage son all alone, I did it! Thus, I got me a job. I began working as a waitress in a Sushi restaurant. However, even though I thought that having a job would cause things to change, it really didn't. Here is where I realized that most people in this generation are suffering from Narcissistic Disorder and that no matter how hard I tried to please people, in general, most people, at least in my life experience, will never be satisfied. In my life experience, I will never be good enough, and there is no winning for me. If I work a lot outside of the home, I am a horrible mother for neglecting my son and leaving him alone and if I don't have a job, I am a horrible mom for not providing for my son. This is just how the system is set up and this is something that I just had to learn to accept.

In this huge house, I worked really hard for my mother's friend. I spring cleaned her entire three-bedroom home, I constantly cleaned up her huge patio that had a lot of work to be done, I would accompany her to do errands and groceries, I even went as far as giving her massages for an entire hour because she had a lot of pain in her bones and hips. But just like it always happened to me, in her mind, she was helping me, and I was just a burden to her. Just how it happened to me over and over, my son and I cleaned up all the fallen leaves from a very large tree that stood on front of her home and we filled up huge garbage bags with these leaves, and took hours to get the job done, yet she told me I don't do anything and that I only cleaned up three leaves.

I heard her tell her friends that I was lazy and that I didn't help her at all and that how can I be so lazy and that she was never like that and on and on she bragged about how hard she worked all her life and what a shameful person I was. Oh, I was so hurt and wounded! My son would witness to all this unfairness and he began to hold a grudge against people. Especially the Christians, because they were the ones who were helping me with one hand and claiming that they were holy and then they were devouring me and exploiting me with the other hand. My son started to dislike the Christians and began to tell me they were all hypocrites! My friend's mom was a devout Catholic and went to church every single Sunday. My son thought that Christians and Catholics were all the same. He told me that I was the only one who ever gave him a real testimony of a true follower of Christ. But because of how bad of a testimony everyone had given my son, I never wanted to take him to any church anymore. Even though by now God had pulled me out of all churches. But I knew that I definitely didn't want my son to continue to experience all these terrible testimonies, because I was afraid that he would turn against God.

For when ye offer your gifts, when ye make your sons to pass through the fire, ye pollute yourselves with all your idols, even unto this day: and shall I be enquired of by you, O house of Israel? As I live, saith the Lord God, I will not be enquired of by you. And that which cometh into your mind shall not be at all, that ye say, We will be as the heathen, as the families of the countries, to serve wood and stone. As I live, saith

the Lord God, surely with a mighty hand, and with a stretched out arm, and with fury poured out, will I rule over you. And I will bring you out from the people, and will gather you out of the countries wherein ye are scattered, with a mighty hand, and with a stretched out arm, and with fury poured out. And I will bring you into the wilderness of the people, and there will I plead with you face to face. Ezekiel 20:31-35

In the middle of all this, Richard came back into my life wanting to be with me. But I was terrified of all the things I had experienced with him and his mom and friend, and I begged God to let me separate from him. I just didn't think we would ever work out as a couple, even though I knew he really liked me. I thought that my character had been pruned by God for twenty years by now and he had just begun the pruning process. I wanted someone who was more mature in the spirit. Someone who didn't say bad words when speaking and who didn't disrespect me when they disagreed with me. I wanted someone who was really surrendered to God and didn't like the things of this world. Because that was the spiritual level that I was in. I had been secluded for years by now. I didn't watch any TV with violence or bad words or sex scenes or immorality. I didn't listen to secular music either. God had even taken away from me the desire to dress too sexy or to wear make up or to dye my hair. I had been completely stripped from the worldly things and I didn't even feel any need to go out and socialize with anyone. I was too focused on surviving all these narcissistic people He had placed in my life to rule over me. I was too busy working on trying to get out of my situation without sacrificing my son and his safety and mental health. I was too busy trying to stay holy so that Satan didn't devour me for all the things I had been doing against him and his kingdom. I didn't want to date a guy who was not in my same spiritual level or above it. I knew that anyone that I would marry would become my head and that I would have to submit to him, thus I wanted someone that could help me become holier and who would not defile me with words, but instead cleanse me with his words.

I was still writing to my online boyfriend and hoping that he would show up. But he would not! I was expecting him to come back in my life, I thought that God was going to bring me a husband that was equipped as a Pastor or a teacher of the word of God is. However, Richard kept on being very persistent and since things with my friend's mother were not so great, I started to look forward to getting away with Richard. Even though we would still have very scary fights, I would go out with him from time to time to just escape the situation that once again, I found myself in.

Moreover, I saved up money from my job and desperately prayed to God to help me to get out of this house, cause this lady was going to kill me slowly with her narcissistic abuse. I remember my friend who is her daughter and whom I have known since high school, she used to complain to me about her mother, but I never imagined it was this painful. I remember she used to go through deep depressions during her high school years and now I can clearly see why. I felt so bad for my friend. I could not imagine growing up with a mother like this. My mother was an angel!

After seven months in that house, I decided to move to Atlanta, GA. My son was the one who picked the place and I agreed because it was cheap and near to Hailie, my beloved niece. By now I had allowed myself to get close to Richard again, yet we were still just friends. I would make sure he knew that I only wanted us to be friends. I was terrified of having another relationship and failing at it. I was exhausted from fighting with the whole world. I always felt that my relationship with him was a bit toxic. Thus, he and I were friends, and he actually became my only friend. During all this time, I had been warning everyone in FB and everyone I knew that a tsunami was coming to our city and I thought that we should move up north so that we can have a safer place; since Richard had been hearing my warnings he decided to help me to move to GA and thought that perhaps it would be a good idea for him to have a place to go to just in case a tsunami was to hit the East Coast as so many people have been warning that is to come. Thus, he helped me get an apartment in GA.

CHAPTER 19

ATLANTA, GEORGIA

Richard put the apartment in GA under his name because my credit was bad, and I didn't qualify to have it under my name. I came up with the money for the down payment and first month's rent with my money from the Sushi restaurant. Richard drove us there. However, he only stayed for a day. He said he had to return to Florida to take care of some business and that he will come back soon. Thus, we moved into a three-bedroom apartment all by ourselves. I chose a three-bedroom, because I wanted my son to have his own room, for once. Also, because I wanted Richard and I to sleep in separate rooms since we were still just friends and I didn't want to fall into sexual sin with him. I was terrified of falling into sexual sin with him, since I knew that all the demons that were cast away from me when I had schizophrenia are waiting for me to give them the legality to enter back inside me. Thus, even though it would be more expensive, I chose a three-bedroom apt. so that I would honor God. Also, I was still having faith that my mystery online boyfriend would eventually come into my life. I wasn't sure how this would play out if it actually happened, but I wasn't sure about my relationship with Richard either, since we fought so much.

Furthermore, I put my son in school, and he had to ride a public-school bus every day to get to school. Before we went in there, we had seen very bad reviews about this specific school, but it was in an area that I can afford and there was nowhere else I can go. I was terrified, but I prayed a lot for God to protect him and I had no choice but to have faith and courage that it will be okay. I immediately began applying for jobs and looked very hard for work. I had no money at one point and was literally trapped in my apt without any money or food. My sister sent me a money order, but then Hailie had to be the one to bring me the money because I had no money to go anywhere. I don't know what would have happened to us if my sister and Hailie had not saved the day.

Later, my phone got disconnected and I had no money to pay it and I was waiting to be called from all the jobs I had applied, thankfully, Richard paid my phone from Florida. I had a real hard time getting a job. I had applied everywhere. I called places and I also went on bus, but no one would call me, and time was passing by. I was really scared. I also noticed that Richard was taking long in coming back and I began to have this weird feeling that even though he was telling me he was coming, that he was not coming at all!

Finally, I got hired at an Italian restaurant. I noticed that many men worked there and only two women were there working. I found that a bit strange, but I paid not much thought to it. I was supposed to get trained for three days by these two women. One of the women was the girlfriend of the manager and the other one was a Mexican woman who had been there for decades and was like the right hand "man" to the owner. When the Mexican woman was training me, I thought she was very nice, complementing my looks and my body and talking about how she longed to lose weight. She began teaching me about packing the meals and serving the guest and a lot of those things, but she neglected teaching me about how to work the computer. The next day, I got the other woman to train me and she also trained me in everything except the computer. Then on the third day, I ended up finding out the hard way that I was supposed to be an expert in the computer by now and was not. Everyone began complaining about my orders from the computer being wrong and just like that, they let me go. I had met a guest in this restaurant that had been nice to me. His name was Mike. He had given me his business card and offered help if I needed it.

The day I was let go, I walked home which was really far, I walked around weeping and weeping with no consolation. I was in complete despair and tired from my journey. I couldn't understand why they would expect me to know the computer work, when none of the women in there had really trained me in the computer. As I was walking home crying, people would stare at me. I had a homeless woman who looked really messed up, come up to me and ask me for help, but she only made me cry harder. I told her that I was sorry but that I had no money. In the midst of my agony, I actually felt really sorry for her. I remember a man on a bike saw me crying and he screamed out really loud:

"God has your back!" I was encouraged a bit by his words, but I continued to cry. When I got home, I called Mike and he said to me: "Desiree, God's got your back! Don't worry, He is with you!" I cried so hard when I heard him tell me that!

He then told me that he knew I would not stay in that job. He said that those women in that restaurant were jealous of me and that he actually witnessed the Mexican woman talking really bad about me in the kitchen to all the staff and turning everyone against me. I was so hurt! Why do women hate me so much everywhere I go? Why are women so competitive and so envious? That is all I can think. Furthermore, I went out and looked for work all over again, on bus. I once again applied everywhere. Meanwhile, my son got into a fight in school, he also got really sick with fever and the flu, most of our neighbors were high on weed in our apartment complex, and my place smelled as if we were smoking weed also. There was always ghetto music with profanity coming into our room from the people who lived above us and we were living without any furniture whatsoever. We had a three-bedroom apartment with an air mattress in one of the rooms. We would sit on the floor to eat and we would try to feel happy.

One day I decided to go to this huge church event in the middle of Atlanta. It was a gathering of all the churches around the area in a huge stadium. I decided to go with my son to this event because I just felt the need to congregate. It had truly been a long time since I went to a Christian gathering and after all I had been through, I thought maybe this will help me. As my son and I were waiting for the same bus, we usually rode, in the middle of a sunny Sunday afternoon, we saw this SUV car drive by and suddenly make a stop. In a split second, these two men got down and one of them asked us if we were from here, and while one of them was finishing his question to us, the other one was pointing a gun to my face! I was stunned in shear fear, yet it didn't stop the words: "I rebuke you in the name of Jesus" from coming out of my mouth, after he told me: "Give me your purse, "you f#@$@% bi%$#!"

Suddenly I felt how he ripped off my huge purse from my arm and both men ran out with it and got in their cars and took off! I was shattered! Even though the Lord had mercy, because they didn't kid nap us or kill us, and they didn't see the pouch bag that was wrapped around my waist, which had all the important things in it. They only robbed a small umbrella, my lady pads for the period and some leather gloves for the cold weather. However, they took my peace of mind with them. I was shaken to the core by them doing this to me. I didn't know at first if I should call the cops, or what should I do? I decided to stay and wait for the bus and still attend the church event. Why should I let those thugs ruin my Sunday afternoon even more, they already violated me, now they are going to punish us in a home with no furniture in it, doing nothing but thinking about what just happened? No, I was going to church and try to forget about what just happened. And thus, we went to the event. My son was also in shock about all of this. I find it quite interesting that I didn't really put oil on both of us every single day before leaving the house, but that day, since we were going so far, I anointed my son and I with oil and prayed before leaving the place and right after we were robbed!

Then when I had to take the subway to get to the stadium, I started to feel fear when I would see men that looked like the ones whom just robbed us. We went to the church event and then came back home. There is a very high crime rate in Atlanta GA, and one day, in one of the jobs I had, 7 different women were robbed in the same parking lot behind my job.

I was working two part time jobs, one in a store called Brooks Brothers in the mall in Downtown Atlanta and another job in a fast food restaurant close to the apt. I would have preferred one full time job, but that is not so easy to get for people like me. Much time had passed before I was hired again, and I was now behind in my rent. My friend Mike ended up lending me one month's rent which was $1,400 with the late fees. This was a miracle from the Lord, because no one lends no one that amount of money without knowing them too long. Yet Mike said to me that he knew God wanted him to do this and so he did! He bought me some more months in there. By now I already knew that Richard was not going to come to stay with us and that I had to tackle this challenge all by myself. I sought help everywhere, I tried charity places, but there really isn't much help out there for people like me. Is very hard to get help. I was working two jobs and hoping that I can catch up and pay my debts, but it was not possible.

Unfortunately, one day I got a phone call from my son at work, he was crying and saying that all our things were thrown outside of our place and that he can't get into the apt. either. He was outside on front of everyone, with all our things on the floor crying and waiting for me to get home from work. The saddest thing was that he had been calling me all day long, but my phone was on silent and I was busy working too even notice. The people in the neighborhood ended up stealing his expensive guitar that his father had given him, and his really expensive camera that his father gave him, both things had been birthday gifts to him from his father and both things had cost $600 each. They stole my book bags that had a lot of expensive books from college and a bunch of other things. This was not fair at all, because the people in the rental office had said to me that if they were going to evict us, they would place a twenty-four-hour eviction notice on our door, but they didn't do that, they never warned us and just like that they humiliated my young son on front of his young friends and had him sit there with all of our things thrown on the floor as if we were some kinds of criminals that deserve this kind of treatment. When I got there, I called the only person I knew that could perhaps help me. Mike! He did! He came and picked us up and drove us to a motel and my sister also helped by sending me money and between her and Mike I was able to survive this whole ordeal. All glory goes to God for providing me with the people that took care of us.

I stayed in the motel for three days. This place was secluded and a bit scary. The smell of cigarettes was suffocating and there were scary looking people roaming around the room whom were really scaring me. But this was the only vacant motel, which we were able to find in such a late notice. We were lucky to find it. After much thinking and praying, even though a man from one of my jobs had offered to take me in and help me get back on my feet, I decided that I would go back to be with Richard. I started remembering all the good things that he has done for me and the many times he has saved me, and even though I was angry with him for staying in Florida and choosing to not move in with me and live in Georgia as we had planned; even though I was upset because I thought that we could have stayed here, had he come, I could not help but think that I am best staying with him. I could not help to think that all the other options on the table were never better than the option of staying with him. I had already lived with a bunch of different people.

I began to think that the rough moments that we experienced together, the fights and the challenges are no different than everything that I had been enduring with everyone else or by myself. I began thinking that even though being with him was very painful at times, being without him was sometimes even more painful. I also thought that even thou sometimes he hurts me, I knew that he loved me deeply. Many of the people that took me in and helped me, also hurt me deeply and instead of seen love in them for me, I saw hatred and envy, something I have never seen in Richard no matter how bad things may get between us. I knew that he loved me and although sometimes is hard for him to show me love, I can sense his love for me is real and always has been. That became priceless to me, after having so much hatred come toward me from almost everyone I knew!

With a very heavy heart I called him and asked him if it would be okay for us to go back to live with him. In a heartbeat, he said yes, and he drove up to Georgia and picked us up. My son was deeply wounded by our departure. He really loved Georgia, in spite of the struggles we had in there. He loved it there very much. He begged me to please not move us back to Florida, but I said that I was very sorry, but we had to move. He wanted to finish his semester in school at least, but sadly we had no money to stay any longer. He only had a month more of school. But unfortunately, I had to take him out of the school. He was very sad and angry by this. He also didn't want to live in Richard's home again. The last impression of us in there was not a good one in his mind. He was extremely upset at God! This was the moment where my son changed. He gave up on God. He felt that God betrayed us. He had the faith that God would get us through in GA and that we would stay there and be stable there. But it didn't turn out that way and my son was just too angry to let it slide. He stopped praying. He stopped believing that prayer worked. He also stopped looking for God altogether. He thought that God didn't really care for us because He would not get us out of this cycle of poverty and mistreatments. By now, my son witnessed everyone around us mistreating me and humiliating me over and over again, and he also experienced some of that treatment himself just for being my son. On the way to Florida from Georgia, my son's heart hardened and closed to God and anything that had to do with Him.

I had to leave him alone. I had to let him go through this without putting any pressure on him or obligating him to look for God. If he felt that way, I could not judge him. I know how painful everything we had gone through had been for him. I had to trust the Lord would heal his wounds and somehow reconcile him back to the Father. I had to have faith that my son would only go through this for a season and that eventually the Lord would turn all of this for our good.

This was also my turning point considering my online mystery boyfriend. I decided I would quit waiting for him after waiting and writing to him for five years. I decided to let him go and to finally admit that he was never coming back in my life and that he was just not the husband that God had for me. Now it was the time to let him go. It was the healthy thing for me to do. I must say that I believe what ended up happening with him was that he got married to the girlfriend he was seen off and on when we first met. I did have dreams where the Lord told me this, but I was in denial about it, because when I had these dreams, I had already been writing to him for years. I remember crying about it very hard and getting very angry, but then I continued to write to him. I told him about these dreams and he never replied to me. But I chose to pretend that he would come to me, because I chose to believe that he was supposed to come since he was the husband God had for me, and I thought that he was not supposed to be with that other woman. I just couldn't stop writing to him, because that was my escape from my dark reality. And even though, I had dreams that he was a married man, I also had dreams about him losing his spiritual battle because of how bad things were between him and that woman. I began praying for him to be okay very hard, since I saw that he was not spiritually okay.

It reminds me of a movie I saw of a true story of a woman who went sailing with her fiancé and then a storm came, and they had an accident in the boat. She rescued her fiancé in the water and spent many days lost at sea, "taking care of him." He was what kept her striving to survive, but when she was found, she realized that she had been hallucinating and the fiancé had died in the sea. (Ironically, her fiancé's name in this film was Richard). But all those days, she was able to bear them, because she "thought" she had him with her. The name of the movie was "Adrift," starring Shailene Woodley, Sam Claflin, Jeffrey Thomas. This is exactly how I felt about my online boyfriend, without that, I don't know if I would be here writing this book today. He literally was my lifeline during those days. Even though I did get upset with God when I realized that He tricked me. But I then tied to imagine what my desert would have felt like, without me expressing my feelings to my online mystery boyfriend? I really could not imagine it, I had no one else to talk to, other than God, throughout all those days. It would have been horrible for me! I also believe God was wisely using my mystery online boyfriend and that entire experience to train me in the prophetic; because of the dreams and revelations that I was writing to him. He was also using this to keep me put in the home I was in, which was no easy thing for me to do, and to keep me not wasting my time dating men and trying to find love, since I thought I had found it and just had to patiently wait for him to return to me. God used this to keep me away from sexual temptation and to help me to tame my wild flesh. He also used this as my therapy to release my sadness and stress and to train me to express myself as blunted as possible without any need of praise or without any fear of rejection. It really did help me to speak my mind in a emotional neutral state. A skill that is essential to acquire for anyone who preaches the truth of our Lord Jesus Christ without sugar coating anything. More importantly, the love God placed in my heart for this man was real and it passionately drove me to get on my knees and pray powerfully for his life, his ministry, his safety, his healing, his liberation and for his return. All that praying was never a waste of time and it always makes me a better person in the end. When we pray for others, we die to our self, that is always a great thing. Thus, as my beautiful friend once told me before he passed away in a car accident in 1995: "Is better to have loved and lost, than to never have loved at all!" Indeed, it is better to have loved and lost, than to never have loved at all!

It was also the time for me to rethink what Richard was constantly telling me, that I was his "wife" from God and that God showed him that I was his wife; thus, after seven months in Georgia we moved back into Richard's home.

CHAPTER 20

BACK IN RICHARD'S HOME

Settling down here once again was once again not an easy task. I put my son back in school and this time I began working with Richard. He has his own company and I was assisting him with everything that he needed for his job. My son now was much older than the last time and we got him a Uber to drive him to school in the morning and he walks home from school afterschool. The fights between his mother and his friend who was still living in there were still strong. His mom used to take out her anger about his friend living in there on me.

Meanwhile, after much fasting and praying, after enduring very turbulent days in Richard's home with all the chaos, as the days went by, Richard and I became closer and closer. Slowly but surely, I found myself in love with him. Richard surely won me over with all his hard work and persistence! He won me over head over hills. I decided to devote my life to God and to him and to my son. And on April 18, 2018 we got married!

My son has come a long way too. He still doesn't commune and pray to God as he used to do, but he has adjusted to this house, he has overcome depression and anxiety. He got into boxing and learned to play the guitar. He was struggling in doing good in school, but now he even is tackling that. He has been getting much better grades as well. I could not be prouder of him! However, it was no easy road for him at all. He worked very hard for his own sake. I also fasted and prayed a whole lot for his recovery. One day he told me God gave him a dream. He said that he had been wondering very hard why was it that God didn't just let me get a real decent job, especially since he knows that I have an Associate's Degree in Psychology. He was wondering why is it that we can't live alone like a lot of single moms live with their children. This was before I was married to Richard. He then said that after pondering upon those things he had this dream. In this dream he had all those things. I had a very good job, we lived alone, and we had a nice place. We owned a nice car and he had his own room and all the things he desired, but when he saw me in the dream, he said that my eyes were stunningly black and I looked like a zombie, as if I was hypnotized. He said he knew I was spiritually dead and that I had given myself over to Satan. He said it was scary to see me that way and that in the dream he didn't want that for me. When he awoke, he shared this dream with me and even thou he mentioned nothing else, I knew that he knew now why it is that God insists in having me live my life the way we live it!

There was a time in Richard's home, that my son was going through so much here that he had decided he would move out with his father, and I have always given him the option to do whatever he wanted concerning moving in with his dad, since I knew how hard it was to endure things with me. Yet at the last minute, he changed his mind and seems to me that he has come up with the conclusion that no matter how hard things may be with me, he is home when he lives with me. I could not feel more flattered!

Throughout all of this, I stayed working for God through FB, until a week before my wedding. The Lord gave me a dream where He showed me that FB was starting to use a technology for mind-control and He ordained me to erase my FB page permanently and stop FB for good. I couldn't be happier to obey. FB became a burden and a job for me, and I did not get paid for doing any of the labor I was doing in it. As soon as I erased my page, I felt the relief and the rest in my spirit. I also saw that my son started feeling better as well. FB is a spiritual portal. All these social media and technologies become spiritual portals. I took a break for a couple of months, but then God instructed me to start uploading YouTube videos about my testimony and sharing my prophetic dreams and revelations that He has given me. Thus, I have been working on my YouTube channel which God named: "Living Waters," through a dream He gave me, and I have been working on my book and Richard loves for me to stay home and focus on prayer and these types of things instead of going out to work with him. His friend ended up being evicted out of this house, but later Richard and him, became best friends again and even though he didn't move him back in with us, they were always together. Sadly, he passed away a couple of months ago.

My life now consists of much prayer and fasting, cleaning and cooking, taping videos on YouTube and writing, and being a wife to Richard and a mother to my son. I also care for my mother in law who recently fell and was injured and needs assistance. I consider myself a very blessed woman and although it was a very painful journey, the wisdom that my son and I received from all these things is priceless. I know that with time God will build up my son's faith again and because of all the trials we endured, I believe he will have great faith because of them. I have faith that God will make him a great and mighty warrior for His kingdom and that he will leave a legacy in this world. I am convinced that the work that God began in my son will bring much fruit when He is finished with it! But for now, my son is living his life like most teenagers these days. And I have learned to let him be and trust God to bring him back to the narrow path someday. Even though my son and I don't attend any church, I spend most of my time in the Presence of all Mighty God and I make sure that I impart upon my son all the wisdom and revelations that God has given me. My son is no longer angry with God, he also acknowledges that He is the truth, the way and the life, but he says that he is not ready to surrender his life for Him the way He sees I have surrendered it. He says he does not wish to be a lukewarm Christian either. He says that if he ever was to be a Christian, he would be an authentic one. But he feels that he is not ready to commit himself that way yet. Of course, I tell him that tomorrow is never promised, I tell him that he should not waste his time either and that Jesus is coming soon, that the rapture is going to happen soon and that judgment upon the world is imminent, but he still doesn't want to repent yet. And of course, I worry about him, of course I pray for his salvation and that God supernaturally protects him. But I must let him be. I have learned that we cannot force anyone to obey God. God doesn't even force any of us either. He gave us all a free will and we must respect that. I let him be! He listens to rock music which I know is satanic, but his father introduced him to it, because his father loves that music and I had to make the decision to allow him to listen to it. I had to make the choice to let him rebel against God on front of me, because if I forced my views upon him, I would have lost him. He would have moved away with his father and then he would be more lost than what he is right now.

At least now, I spend a lot time with him, talking to him and giving him good advice. I have shared my entire life story with him, I have prayed over him as he sleeps, over and over. I have monitored his daily affairs, to make sure he is not doing drugs or crimes or things of that matter. I have been there to cook for him healthy meals so he may be strong and healthy, instead of having him eating fast food meals all the time. I have been there to let him speak to me his mind about his fears and worries and all the things he needs to take out of his chest, so that he doesn't feel the need to do bad things to feel better. I have been there for him to receive love and affection and affirmation so that he doesn't need to be looking for that in all the wrong teenage girls that will break his heart in pieces. I had to compromise some of my beliefs to allow him to be free enough to make him want to stay near me. I also let him watch movies that I know he should not be watching. He knows that I don't approve of them. He is not allowed to watch any pornography or very horror types of films, I do have boundaries. But I had to let him watch the Hollywood movies that have bad words and some sexual and violent content that I disapprove of us watching, just because he needs to be free enough to stay around me.

My husband is also much more liberal than me, and I had to accept him the same way as well. He was a baby in Christ when we met and just as I took a long time to change my ways, and God was patient with my process, I had to be patient with my husband's process as well. Overall, the transformation in my husband's life is quite impressive so far. He was brought up pretty savagely as well and endured much hardship throughout his youth. Thus, he still also watches movies like the ones my son watches, and I had to let him be. I can't be a controlling sergeant in the house and drive everyone crazy trying to force holiness upon all of them. My mother in law also watches soap operas in Spanish which are demonic and not good. But I have to let her be. First of all, that is her house. We live in her place. Second of all, my husband is the head of the house, not me. He pays the bills and I am the homemaker. Third of all, my son would not be better off or holier living with his father. And if I tried to impose my rules upon him, he would have moved in with his father a long time ago, to be alone most of the time, because his father works, and he would be listening to rock music and watching Hollywood movies all the time but without any guidance at all. That seemed like a much worst deal for me.

I believe that the Lord Himself is the One who instructed me to allow this to happen. He has taught me to take my frustration on my knees and pray and fast about all of them. I pray and fast daily for all of them to get convicted that without holiness we will not see the Lord. I have the faith that the day will come, that they will feel the same way I feel, when they see sinful things on TV or when they hear music that offends our Lord. They also say bad words. I had to learn to endure this. I sometimes plead with them to please stop, but I can't be a control freak either, because there would be no peace in the house. The biggest challenge for me has been to stay holy myself in the middle of all of them. I have been living this way all my life. I have always been surrounded by people that don't see anything wrong with saying bad words or listening to secular music or watching regular Hollywood movies and TV. I have always been under their rulership as well, because most of my life, God has assigned me to be the homemaker in the house. He has assigned me to submit to all of them, to serve them, and to pray for them. He has assigned me to preach to them the gospel and to endure the mockery and the humiliation that comes from not having my own money or paying the bills.

Concerning my son, he must submit to me, and I do have rules that he needs to abide by. I just made sure that I gave him space to breath. In a different world, I would have been stricter with him in certain things, but because of the crazy circumstances we had been enduring and because of the level of attacks that we had to constantly face from people in our lives, I had to let him relax and I had to be more flexible with him. My goals with him rapidly changed, from aspiring that he makes straight A's in school and becomes a holy Christian, to just wishing for him to want to live. Unfortunately, because of all the negative situations we had to endure, because of the way our society has become, my goals with my son became that he survives all the madness around us, without going insane. My goal became to try to make him as happy as possible so that he doesn't kill himself. My goal became to help him to navigate through the chaos we were in and to still desire to live.

In weekdays, he is not allowed to come home too late, and thankfully, for me, he comes with me and Richard in the weekends. Richard has made it possible for my son to not have the need to be going to clubs or parties or things of that nature, because we are always going to fun places with my son and Richard's son and daughter. Thus, I don't even have to set any rules for my son during the weekends because he spends them with us. Thus, even though I have compromised some of my beliefs with my son, it has paid off, because he is doing well in general and in comparison to most teenage boys nowadays. And if you would know the details of the pain my son has endured through his childhood, you would know that this is a huge miracle from God. And even though he is not sitting in a church every Sunday or Saturday and listening to a long sermon, he gets to listen to the truth and the word of God daily with me at home. God has been training him through me even better than in a church. We do engage in very deep conversations about God and the devil, about heaven and hell and about souls and the human race. We constantly find ourselves analyzing our lives and those we live with and we try to understand the world around us together. Like a teacher and a student would do in a classroom setting.

One time, I came home and shared an experience to my son that I had encountered in the public bus that I sometimes use to get around. I told him about this lady that was in the bus and she seemed to be very mentally ill. I told him about how she was sitting across of me and was threatening me with her hands and facial expression. She was telling me that she was going to "$%^& me up!" and she would point her hands at me and looked really angry at me. I described this event to him and we both were marveled by it and that was the end of that.

A couple of weeks later, my son and I were taking the same bus back home and behold, the lady that I had mentioned to him was sitting right next to me on the other side of the bus. That day the bus was packed with people and my son and I had to separate, he sat behind the lady. I had not noticed her. My son had never seen her before, but she was acting weird as I had described to him that she would act, thus, he asked me very discretely: "Mom, is she the one you were telling me about?" As I saw her, I froze in fear, because this woman would give me the chills! And not just me, I noticed that everyone around her in the bus looked afraid of her as well. I told my son, yes that is the woman and then I turned my head around and just looked to the other side, hoping that she would not notice me. But she did. And she began to act out again, but this time was much more intense. She began talking loud to me. She was sounding very angry and as if she knew me. I was embarrassed and didn't know what to do. I began to pray. I was curious as to why no one in the bus would tell her to be quiet. She was really loud. But the whole bus, seemed to be as frozen in fear as I felt. She had this evil presence within her that was tangible, and the anger that came behind her words were too strong for anyone to dare to say anything. I decided to get up and move out of the place I was sitting in, because it looked as if she was about to hit me. My son was ready to defend me, because he was sitting behind her and I can tell he was ready to hold her down if she dared to hit me. I moved toward the front of the bus and never looked at her. But my son later told me that her eyes followed me through the entire process, and she would not stop telling me off! People were starting to look at her and then at me and I can see their confusion in their eyes about what was happening. I kept saying to myself that I was to not look at her, just ignore her the whole time. I was looking out the window and praying inside me.

I was trying to discern what it was that she was saying and behold to my surprise, she was uttering my life. She was saying all the things people that hate me love to criticize me and say about me. Word by word, she began uttering the same sayings everyone that hates me tells me. She said that I didn't want to work, and that I lived from everyone else. That I lived from my parents, then from my grandmother, then from my boyfriend, and she even spoke about Richard. She was saying a lot of things that were very hurtful to me, when other people would say them to me and then I suddenly heard her say: "It has been over twenty years already!" and she stopped talking and just stayed silently and intensely staring at me. I can feel her stare and after I heard that last statement, I just knew that the one talking to me, was not that woman, that woman was just a host body to the spirit of schizophrenia that had been cast out of my body over twenty years ago exactly! I was liberated in 1998 and this happened in 2018. I was so shocked when I heard her say that, and I felt so much emotion after hearing those words, that all my fear left me, and I decided to turn around and stare at that demon straight in his eyes. Thus, I did just that! But after a long time passed and neither of us would blink, I turned around again and started to ignore her again. She then started saying more bad words and calling me a b@#$% and finally I arrived at my bus stop and left.

My son was speechless. He knew that all that was spiritual. He knew that demons were the ones that said all those things. He knew that she was uttering my life and the bad things that everyone always said about me. He knew that twenty years ago, I was liberated from schizophrenia! He knew that she seemed so angry as if she knew me and that she only had been talking to me, out of all the people that were in there. He knew that, that was extremely strange. Why did she choose me to torment? Why was she so mad at me? My son knows all the things I have done for God and he saw firsthand just how upset Satan is with me. She threatened me again, just as she did the last time that I ran into her. But this time, my son saw the whole thing. My son knew that when I had been ill with Schizophrenia, I had people randomly tell me messages like how this lady just did in the bus. Because I had shared this information with him in the past. Now my son saw that everything that I had been telling him is true. Now my son saw that without a shadow of a doubt, everything I have ever taught him and shared with him is true. He told me that now he really believed me. We both stayed in total shock for a while, concerning what took place in the bus. And even though it was very scary, and she insulted me, cuss at me and it was humiliating to me, I am very glad it happened, and I am very glad that my son was there to witness it. I feel that God allowed this to happen so my son's faith in Him can increase and so that he can see the spiritual battle we are in. And for me it was a blessing to see that I am really upsetting Satan and, I got to see that all those people who were always criticizing me and saying those awful things about me were only being used by demons to hurt me and that they need to repent and be delivered from them. It was a blessing and I am so glad that we don't have a car and use the bus, and that we were able to experience this, because my son's own words were that he will never forget that day and that lady and what happened in that bus. In his own words, he uttered: "I now know that God is real!" I know this will help him in the future. The moral of this story is, that even though my son is not in a church or in any Christian youth group, the Lord is still building his faith and character through my life and through the experiences he has with me around.

Also, even though I did not marry a Pastor or a teacher of the word of God, I married a business man that made it possible for me to be the best mother I could possibly be, by letting me stay home and focus on educating my son with the truth and in love, by giving me the time and the provision to cook and feed him healthy meals, by giving me the time to take good care of him when he got sick and by giving me the time to keep him entertained so that he doesn't get into trouble. I married a business man that believed in me and in my projects and financed most of my work on FB, he paid for most of the Documentary that I worked on which is called: "American Hijack" by Film Maker Frank Panico, he financed all my YouTube videos, and he made this book possible as well because of maintaining my son and I while I stay home and work on it and he is the one who will pay the thousands of dollars it takes, for this book to be published. He also made it possible for me to be the best wife that I can possibly be, and he even helped me lose weight, by giving me healthy meals and the time to work out and rest properly.

He may not be the "Pastor or teacher of the word of God, type of man" that I was expecting, but he made all my dreams come true! He also takes my son and I to very cool places and gives us a glimpse of a good life from time to time. He accepted my son as his own and provided for him everything my son desires. My husband is not perfect, but he is the perfect one for me. It hasn't always been easy and before we were married, there were times I thought of leaving him, but through much prayer and love, we overcame our differences. He proved his love for me is real, not with words but with actions and sacrifices. He was the only one there for me when everyone in my life left me! Behind all the rubble that I saw in his character that sometimes would scare me, I found a beautiful heart of gold. He is my Boaz from the book of Ruth in the Bible and my best and dearest friend. Our relationship is still not perfect and we definitely have many areas to work hard at fixing; but I have learned to receive all of God's blessings with much persecutions. By now, I am very well trained in seen the good in everything and praying over the bad things I see. I have learned to thank God for everything and to trust Him in those things that are beyond my control. If I had decided to wait for the "perfect husband" to come my way, I will remain single forever. Besides, I am very well aware that I am far from perfect myself.

As long as God is the One wanting for Richard to be my husband, then I must choose to trust Him to get us through all the trials and hardships. God has certainly proven to me that Richard is the one that He chose for me to be with. He gave me many dreams to reveal to me that I was not to leave him when I contemplated leaving him. At times, there were many circumstances in my life, which always pointed out that God was closing every other door of an option for me to go away from Richard. And when there were other times where I did have the option to leave Richard, the Lord would reveal to me that it was not His will for me to leave him. Richard also prayed a lot for God to remove me out of his life, if I was not the woman of God that he needed. Richard is a praying man, and he indeed prayed a lot for us to stay together or to separate if God so willed. Richard and I both have had our share of horrible relationships and we are both pretty traumatized by them, thus we were both really serious in what it was that God thought about us being a couple. Consequently, God has most certainly proven and confirmed to me that Richard is the one that He chose for me and ordained me to love him unconditionally and to pray for him, to serve him in everything he needs, to be submissive to him, to be faithful and loyal and to cover his flaws and sins with love and prayers and that is what I have been doing.

And above all things have fervent charity/love among yourselves: for charity/love shall cover the multitude of sins. 1 Peter 4:8

Richard is known by name, all over our neighborhood by many homeless and needy people. He helps everyone in need and gives them money and food and comforts them with words. He loves to help the poor and the needy like no one I have ever met. He is a generous, giving man! He loves his two children that he has from previous relationships and his step children that he raised as his own. He also loves and cares for his elderly mother. He is definitely a family man. He is always working hard to provide for all of us and is always looking for ways to bring the family together and to create loving and fun memories together. I don't know what my life would have been like without Richard in it. I was always trying so hard to balance my life and no matter what I did or how hard I worked, I was never able to balance my life. It was only when Richard came along that finally, I found balance in my life. There was no other way for me to do it. I needed a husband. I needed a good provider to allow me to live in a balanced manner. If God would have never brought me my husband, I would most probably have lost my son to his father and I would most probably be stuck in secular jobs that would have stopped me from working on the projects I just mentioned I did. My son would have grown up all by himself as well. His father is always working; thus, my son would have probably grown up just as the majority of us grew up. Alone, and involved with wrong things and hanging out with the wrong people. I am not saying my son is a saint, because he is not, but he is definitely not as bad as most of the youth I grew up with was, including myself.

God was faithful and rewarded me with a great husband and a great new family! Even though He provided for me in ways that I didn't understand, and even though it required that I humble myself in a level I never thought was possible to do, I now can clearly see that He knew very well what He was doing and that it was worth all the pain and the humiliation I had to endure! Even though I still aspire for my husband and for my son to live a holier life and to surrender certain things to the Lord, I believe that in God's perfect timing, we will be living our lives in a much higher level of surrender to our Lord and that we will be in His holy and perfect will. I have the faith that as the judgments of God continue to be poured out upon the earth, it will shake up the people and a revival will come with the judgments and we will continue to grow in faith, knowledge and fear of the Lord and we will reach our fullest potential in the Lord and that all this process was a learning experience for all of us. I am forever thankful and honored to serve such an awesome God. To Him be all the glory, the honor and the power, Amen!

This is a passage from the book: "He Came To Set The Captives Free, by Dr. Rebecca Brown. "Elaine Talks: During my years in The Brotherhood I was carefully trained, and I in turn trained others, how to infiltrate and destroy the various Christian churches. Satan's goal is to make every Christian church like the church of Laodicea described by our Lord Jesus Christ in **Revelation 3:15-16 I know thy works, that thou art neither cold nor hot: I would thou wert cold or hot. So then because thou art lukewarm and neither cold nor hot, I will spue thee out of My mouth."** Churches are full of passive people who never bother to read or study the Bible, who "Having a form of godliness, but denying the power thereof..." as so well described in 2 Timothy 3:15, are not a threat to Satan. We were taught a basic eight-point plan of attack that could be adapted to whatever denomination of church we were sent to. The fact that most all high ranking satanists regularly attend Christian churches should not be a surprise to anyone. That is, anyone who takes the time to read God's word. We Christians are very clearly warned that Satan's attack will come from within the churches--especially in times of prosperity. (Chapter 17, Destruction of Christian Churches, page 233. He Came To Set The Captives Free by Dr. Rebecca Brown).

This a passage from the book: "The Spiritual Man by Watchman Nee". "How lamentable to find modern-day Christians achieving no progress in their spiritual walk after several years, nay, even after decades. These moreover are filled with amazement if they find some who do enter upon a life of the spirit after a number of years. They consider it most unusual, not aware it is but normal--the regular growth of life. How long have you believed in the Lord? Are you spiritual yet? We should not become aged babes, grieving the Holy Spirit and suffering loss ourselves. All regenerated ones should covet spiritual development, permitting the Holy Spirit to rule in every respect so that in a relatively short period He may be able to lead us into what God has provided for us. We should not waste time, making no progress. (Chapter 2, The Fleshly or Carnal Believer, page 85, The Spiritual Man by Watchman Nee).

To all of those prosperity preachers who love to use the passage from **Malachi 3:10** to teach your congregations to pay you your tithes, if you are going to use this verse to receive tithes, comparing yourselves to the Levites, which this verse is referring to, you need to also apply to your lives the regulation that God gave the Levites about not having any inheritance with the Israelites. You need to live humble lives and depend solely on the tithes and offerings of your people and not work in secular jobs. Levites were in the same category as the widows, the orphans, the strangers, the poor and the needy.

> **When thou hast made an end of tithing all the tithes of thine increase the third year, which is the year of tithing, and hast given it unto the Levite, the stranger, the fatherless, and the widow, that they may eat within thy gates, and be filled. Deuteronomy 26:12**

They lived very humble lives and were not working in anything other than the Lord's service. **Number 18.**

> **Repent ye therefore, and be converted, that your sins may be blotted out, when the times of refreshing shall come from the presence of the Lord; And he shall send Jesus Christ, which before was preached unto you: Whom the heaven must receive until the times of restitution of all things, which God hath spoken by mouth of all his holy prophets since the world began. Act 3:19-21**

THE END!

SALVATION PRAYER

If you haven't come to our Lord Jesus Christ/Yeshua Hamashiac yet, and you wish to do that today, repeat this prayer out loud:

"Lord Jesus/Yeshua, I come before Your presence, recognizing that I am a sinner; please forgive me for all of my sins. I recognize that You died on the cross of Calvary for my sins and that You resurrected on the third day to give me eternal life. I recognize that You are the Word/God, (John 1:14) that became flesh and suffered my penalty for sin so that I may be saved. I thank You for Your sacrifice and I receive by faith Your gift of salvation. Holy Spirit please come into my heart and guide me to all truth. I receive you as my Lord and Savior. I renounce my body of iniquity, the world and Satan. I pray that You write my name in the Book of eternal life. I cover my life with the blood of the lamb and pray that You help me to take care of my salvation with fear and tremble. Philippians 2:12. Please send your angels to encamp around me and I put on the whole armor of God. I put on the helmet of salvation, the breastplate of righteousness, the shield of faith, the sword of the Spirit, the belt of the truth and the shoes of the gospel of peace. Thank you for saving me and for guiding me, in Jesus/Yeshua's mighty name, I pray. Amen.

If you prayed this prayer, I want to welcome you to the body of Christ. I earnestly pray that you stand firm in

His truth and that you overcome all the wiles of the enemy. May the Lord grant you supernatural peace, protection and wisdom in your journey with Him and may you fulfill the desires of our Lord's heart in your life. God bless you abundantly and may we see each other in heaven someday. Thank you for reading my story, it was my honor to serve you and to serve our Lord Jesus Christ/Yeshua Hamashiac.

Reference: Santa Biblia/Holy Bible Edicion Bilingue, Bilingual Edition. Reina Valera 1960. RVR 1960/King James Version.

WOUNDED

Like a roaring lion tearing my spirit apart in pieces, I feel my spirit bleed internally. Never have I experienced such a spiritual battle as real as this one. Pain as profound and deep as the oceans: Lord, I praise You for this battle for You are Powerful. The deeper the pain the higher the comfort. Thank You for making me go through experiences where I don't desire to be. Thus, the lessons in them are as fascinating as the deepest seas. The adventure of finding You through it all is as exciting as the ultimate pleasure. As the raging waves come closer, and the sharks are surrounding all around me, I glance up at the doorway to heaven and with blood tears I scream Your lovely Name, which is above all names: Jesus Christ my Savior.

Swimming with Your Majesty to the deepest part of the sea, not wanting to really go, but may Your will be done. I find myself looking at things I have never imagined I would see. Understanding concepts, I'd never thought were real. Realizing how real You are and how everything truly revolves around You oh Lord. For You are the wisest teacher I have ever known. The most skillful Lord of lords. So many details to Your great Majesty. Making You so fascinating, I am in love with You: I love You so much God!

Thank You for Your discipline, thank You for all Your tests, thank You for all the pain that has made me call Your lovely name. Thank You for placing Your precious hands on my wounded heart and taking all the blood toward God. Showing me what You did for me on the Calvary cross was the ultimate prize a painful lesson of love would receive value of life. I appreciate everything about You. Please always comfort me and help me go through my journey. As a servant of the Lord enduring hardship as a good soldier of Jesus Christ. All glory, honor and power be to You my Lord!

And they overcame him by the blood of the Lamb, and by the word of their testimony; and they loved not their lives unto the death. Revelation 12:11

www.testimoniesofhell.com

Miami Dade College

Has conferred on

Desiree Carrasquillo

the degree of

Associate in Arts

and all the rights and privileges thereunto appertaining.

In Witness Whereof, this diploma, duly signed, has been issued and the seal

of the College affixed.

Issued by the District Board of Trustees of Miami Dade College

upon recommendation of the Faculty of the College at Miami, Florida

this month of May, A.D. 2010

Chairman, District Board of Trustees

President

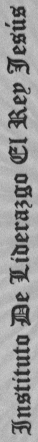

Instituto De Liderazgo El Rey Jesús

Miembro del Florida Council for Private Colleges, Inc.
Tallahassee, Florida

Otorga el presente

Certificado en Fundamentos Crístíanos

a

Desíree Carrasquillo

Por haber culminado satisfactoriamente estudios en Principios y Formación de Líder Cristiano

En testimonio de lo cual, sella este certificado con nuestra firma

Dado en Miami-Dade, Florida el 26 de junio de 2010

John Laffitte

Dr. John Laffitte, Vice-Presidente Ejecutivo

Guillermo Maldonado

Apóstol Guillermo Maldonado, Presidente

DISCHARGE SUMMARY

DATE OF ADMISSION: 5/29/96   DATE OF DISCHARGE: 6/6/96

ATTENDING PHYSICIAN: M. GONZALEZ-BLANCO MD

RESIDENT PHYSICIAN: DR. LOSSADA

ADMITTING DIAGNOSIS:

AXIS I.   PSYCHOSIS NOS. RULE OUT SCHIZOPHRENIA CHRONIC PARANOID TYPE.
AXIS II. UNSPECIFIED.
AXIS III. DENIES
AXIS IV. PROBLEM WITH PRIMARY SUPPORT.

DISCHARGE DIAGNOSIS:

AXIS I.   SCHIZOAFFECTIVE DISORDER, RULE OUT SCHIZOPHRENIA CHRONIC TYPE.
AXIS II. UNSPECIFIED.
AXIS III. DENIED
AXIS IV. POOR FAMILY SUPPORT.
AXIS V.   FAIR.

HISTORY OF PRESENT ILLNESS: THE PATIENT IS A 19-YEAR-OLD WHITE LATIN FEMALE
WITH NO PAST PSYCHIATRIC HISTORY WHO WAS BAKER ACTED TO CRISIS JACKSON
MEMORIAL HOSPITAL DUE TO DEPRESSED MOOD, AGGRESSIVE EPISODES AND BIZARRE
BEHAVIOR. AT THE MOMENT OF ADMISSION THE PATIENT CLAIMS TO BE VIRGIN MARY
REINCARNATION, AND THAT SHE IS BEING CHASED BY WITCHES.

MENTAL STATUS: THE PATIENT ALERT AND ORIENTED TIMES THREE, WITH SAD MOOD,
AND AFFECT CONGRUENT. RELIGIOUS AND PARANOID DELUSIONS. NO AUDITORY OR
VISUAL HALLUCINATIONS. NO FLIGHT OF IDEAS, NO HOMICIDAL OR SUICIDAL
IDEATIONS, AGITATED TO THE POINT THAT RESTRAINTS WERE NEEDED TO REDIRECT
BEHAVIOR.

FAMILY HISTORY: MOTHER IS ACTUALLY SICK, SUFFERING FROM BREAST CANCER.
FATHER IS AN ALCOHOLIC.

(CONTINUED ON NEXT PAGE)

CPSIA information can be obtained
at www.ICGtesting.com
Printed in the USA
LVHW040922170520
655737LV00002B/123

9 781645 698449